THE NEW-FASHIONED PARENT

Also by Eleanor Berman
THE COOPERATING FAMILY

THE NEW-FASHIONED PARENT

How to Make Your Family Style Work

by Eleanor Berman

PRENTICE-HALL, INC., *Englewood Cliffs, New Jersey*

The New-Fashioned Parent:
How to Make Your Family Style Work
by Eleanor Berman
Copyright © 1980 by Eleanor Berman
All rights reserved. No part of this book may be
reproduced in any form or by any means, except
for the inclusion of brief quotations in a review
without permission in writing from the publisher.
Address inquiries to Prentice-Hall, Inc.,
Englewood Cliffs, N.J. 07632
Printed in the United States of America
Prentice-Hall International, Inc., London
Prentice-Hall of Australia, Pty. Ltd., Sydney
Prentice-Hall of Canada, Ltd., Toronto
Prentice-Hall of India Private Ltd., New Delhi
Prentice-Hall of Japan, Inc., Tokyo
Prentice-Hall of Southeast Asia Pte. Ltd., Singapore
Whitehall Books Limited, Wellington, New Zealand

Library of Congress Cataloging in Publication Data
Berman, Eleanor, date
The new-fashioned parent.
Includes index.
1. Family—United States. 2. Marriage—United
States. 3. Social role. 4. Children—Management.
I. Title.
HQ536.B46   301.42'0973   79-25728
ISBN 0-13-613406-8

Contents

66939

For my mother and father, the very best of families

Acknowledgments

I want to express my sincere thanks to the many men and women who shared their experiences and thoughts with me, and I am especially grateful to the following, who were so generous in sharing their professional expertise: Dr. Vidal S. Clay, Mary Corcoran, John Demos, Stephen Dworkin, Jeanne Ellis, Elizabeth Granfield, Carol Feit Lane, Bill Matthews, Jane MacColl, Margaret Murta, Dr. Nancy D. Stevens.

I

The Changing Family

The time: 3:15 P.M. The place: Suburban Lane, Anytown, U.S.A. The school bus has just stopped at the corner, discharging a dozen noisy youngsters who are running and skipping toward home. Behind them comes the high-school crowd, walking more slowly, arms laden with books, chatting and laughing as they stroll.

It's a familiar American scene. Time was when we could have predicted what would follow. At the door of each home would be Mom, waiting to welcome her youngsters with milk and cookies, to listen to the trials and triumphs of the day, then to send the children off to their friends and their play while she returned to her job of making dinner in preparation for Dad's return from work.

A predictable and pleasant scene, to be sure. But these have not been predictable times. Many of these children won't find their mothers at home. More than half the mothers of America's school-age children have gone to work.

1

In some of these homes, no father will be coming home to dinner. The divorce rate has doubled in the past decade, leaving ten million children living at least part of their growing-up years in a single-parent home.

It seems, in fact, that the "typical" American family is vanishing. Of the 56 million households counted in the 1976 census, only 3.3 million fit the old formula of a married man supporting a wife and two children. In 1977, for the first time since the government began collecting this kind of data, it was decreed that husbands would no longer automatically be designated as heads of households, for it was found that in more than half of our households, more than one paycheck was coming in.

The family *is* changing, in ways so basic that none of us are completely unaffected. Some even wonder if family life as we've known it will be able to survive at all.

The experts are concerned. Historians are delving into the past, seeking insight into our puzzling present. College courses studying the role of the family have burgeoned. The rise of the "nuclear family" has been explored, its impact argued pro and con. Books have been written, conferences on the family called for by everyone from the President of the United States to NOW, the National Organization for Women that worked so hard to help women break out of their homes.

Meanwhile, as the debates go on, as conferences confer and theories are proposed, millions

2

of families on America's "Suburban Lanes" and "City Avenues" haven't got time to wait for opinions from the experts. They are much too busy leading their own everyday lives and worrying about the same kinds of things that have always concerned the family unit: making a living, bringing up happy and healthy children, maintaining strong ties of support and affection between husband and wife, parent and child.

This is a book written for and about those families. It is based on interviews with more than 200 people focusing on how families can and have adapted to meet the demands of the day.

Some of the people I met with were professionals who teach or counsel families. More were simply ordinary people, mothers and fathers who were coping with the pressures of the times in their own ways.

From all of them, one message was overwhelming. The family can and does still work for most of us, in spite of the strains upon it in a changing society. What's more, while change can bring upset, it also brings opportunity. In many homes today there is a richer life texture because of some of the shifts that have occurred. As mothers expand their horizons outside the home, many fathers are finding new and more meaningful roles within the family, while children are learning to become more productive members of their households. Single parents have discovered that love and mutual concern are still the ingredients for a warm and happy home, in spite of life's crises.

These families that have successfully weathered some of the traumas of the times have valuable insight to offer. Whether you are a working mother struggling to juggle two jobs, a father hoping to establish closer emotional bonds with your family, a stay-at-home mother feeling out of touch with modern times because of your traditional role, a couple striving for a more meaningful marriage or a parent concerned about bring up children in a time of transition, you will find practical guidance and perhaps a bit of inspiration in the experiences of other families very much like yours.

It is important to hear from these families, because we tend to hear so much about families in difficulty and so little about those families that remain sound in spite of change. As a result of all this negative emphasis, a curious thing has happened: Everyone seems to be feeling slightly uneasy. The majority, those who remain married and maintain a familiar way of life, are wondering if they are out of step with the times. Families who fit the new descriptions of role sharing and changing patterns are feeling their own qualms about leaving ways that society has ordained as right for so long.

intro Families, after all, are groups of individuals who live together. When we talk about the problems of a family, we are talking about the meshing of the needs of its individual members. The system worked neatly when there was a clear-cut division of labor between fathers and mothers, an understanding that the good of the family group came

4

before the ambitions of any one member. As women began moving out of the home, they left a void difficult to fill and made new demands on their men that many found difficult to meet. Changing conceptions of the roles of men and women are affecting almost everyone today, and for the first time there is uncertainty about how much personal sacrifice should be made for the sake of the family.

For parents, this insecurity about their roles has made it harder to bring up children. Fashions in child rearing have always swung back and forth between permissiveness and strictness, but parents in the past could feel reasonably sure about instilling certain universally accepted values in their children. Now we are being told that the old-fashioned ideals may no longer hold true. There is new freedom and equality between the sexes, new options in life-styles. With the old role models in question, mothers and fathers are less sure about what to tell their children even when their own values have not wavered.

There are no easy answers to these dilemmas, yet the family, historically resilient and responsive to the needs of each era, remains healthy in spite of its changes. The more uncertain the world becomes, the more we seem to recognize the importance of enduring ties. A recent poll of Americans bears this out, revealing that four out of five people still choose a happy family life as more important than making a lot of money, having a fulfilling career or developing as an individual.[1]

How best to achieve that happy family life is the question that concerns us, and there is much to be learned from the examples of latter-day "typical" families: the problems they recognize and what they are doing to try to solve them.

There is also a lesson to be learned from families of the past, for ours is not the first generation to be faced with a challenge to the family. The family unit has changed its form many times to respond to the needs of each era. So before we delve into the present, it's helpful to look back to see how we've arrived at where we are today.

II

The Myth of the Typical American Family

"What's to become of the family? Women aren't content to stay at home anymore, there's free-and-easy sex everywhere, young people don't care about their old parents—why no one stays in one place anymore!"

The complaints are familiar, but the date may surprise you. America's first vocal "crisis" of the family occurred in the late 1700s. Nor was that the last time that people noted the decline of the "typical American family." With all the romanticizing that is done about the idea of the family, it came about as a way of life for purely practical reasons and has survived because it has been adaptable, because what is "typical" has changed according to the needs of each era.

Our much-discussed "nuclear family"—the immediate family of husband, wife, and children—

is far from new. It pre-dates American history and may well date all the way back to the caveman. In primitive times, the male-female couple emerged to satisfy the two most basic biological drives: sex and hunger. Physical attraction brought men and women together. When their union produced children, a most efficient division of labor came about. The hunter-father provided food and protection while the mother prepared the food, cared for the children and serviced her husband's sexual needs. Since a hunter's life was nomadic, a constant search for food, his family was small by necessity, no more than the wife and children he could care for and shelter easily.

The introduction of farming changed life's pattern to a more settled existence. Men were still in charge of the food, but it was now provided by fields of crops and herds of animals. Extra hands were welcome and needed.

Women continued to take care of the home and children, and prepare meals, but they also began to develop crafts such as pottery making and weaving, which provided a means of trading for goods the family could not provide for itself. They began teaching these skills to their children, turning the whole family into a working unit.

Large families were now an asset. More laborers meant that more land could be worked and more crafts produced. The family was bound together by their mutual dependence.

The wife was a vital partner in keeping the household running, but the physically stronger male was still the dominant figure. The position of women in early societies can be gathered from reading the Tenth Commandment: "Thou shalt not covet thy neighbor's house, thou shalt not covet thy neighbor's wife ... nor his ox ... nor anything that is thy neighbor's." Women were considered property, along with the house and the cattle. They were passed from father to husband, were not allowed to inherit property, to take part in economic or political life. They could not survive without a man to protect them.

Eventually, as towns began to grow up, the large family groups that had been an advantage in an agricultural society became outmoded once again. On the farm, all the members of the family were producers, but in the city it was usually a father's task to support his family on his wages. Homes were smaller in the city and there was more movement from place to place to find work, so families became smaller and more scattered. And children could no longer depend on learning work skills at home. For the first time, they required special education to prepare them for adult life.

For America's first settlers, however, the hard realities of existence in a brand-new country returned the family to a working unit. Each household was faced with the challenge of clearing land, building a home and providing its own food and clothing. Just as in earliest times, husbands and wives worked as teams, the physically stronger male providing the food and shelter while his wife cooked and preserved the food, and cared for the

9

children. Wives also spun and wove cloth, washed and sewed and mended, made candles and soap and ministered to the sick. There was endless work to be done, inside and outside; tools were crude and human labor was badly needed. So once again, children were economic assets. Families of eight or nine became common.

Home in early America was once again the place where children were trained in vocational skills, but it was not the multigenerational unit that so many people think of as an "extended family." When a couple married, it was assumed that they would set up housekeeping for themselves. The families of both bride and groom contributed what land, housing, money and household goods they could spare to make this possible.

From the earliest days of the nation, the lure of empty land and new opportunity attracted many young people. The portion parents could give was often less than a couple could hope to gain for themselves by moving out to the frontier. It was part of the New World experience that families might be divided, that some elderly parents might be left alone to fend for themselves after their children moved on in search of a better life. Right from the start we have the theme that was to play so important a part in the lives of immigrant families in American history: The young, born and bred in this country, often proved more resourceful in meeting its challenges than their parents.

In spite of their importance, women in colonial days were still very much second-class citizens, expected to honor and obey their husbands. Formal education was largely limited to males. However, women were protected by law from abuse by their husbands, and there is evidence that many women became active in business pursuits, running inns and taverns and managing shops and stores. They seemed to have mixed easily with men in many areas of everyday life.

This informality of life in the New World, with its opportunities for the sexes to mingle, appears to have given rise to a growing tolerance for premarital sex. By checking birth dates against parental wedding dates in public records, historian John Demos reports that by 1750 some one-third to one-half of the brides were going to the altar pregnant.[2]

It is interesting, and perhaps instructive, to see that by the end of the eighteenth century, American family life had been transformed in some of the very ways that people find so alarming today. Young couples were leaving home to seek their fortunes elsewhere, cutting family ties. The possibility that they could leave was eroding parental authority. Women were moving more freely in society and there was a growing permissiveness in the area of sex. There was vocal concern about the future of the family.

The result of these developments was a sharp swing back to more restrictive ways, an attempt to reinstate more rigid discipline and more structured sex standards. Women began to return to their homes, to the task of giving deeper meaning to family life.

The change was more than a matter of values. It was also a response to changing social needs. The hard pioneer life was over. Cities were growing up. There were new opportunities, new chances for building wealth in business. Instead of the cooperative community spirit that had marked the country's early years, the new emphasis was on individualism and competition. In the face of these new challenges, there was a need for traditional moorings, shelter from the stresses and storms of the competitive world. Home and hearth were to be that shelter. And at the center of the home was woman, faithfully tending that hearth.

Nineteenth-century woman had an easier life, but a much more restricted one than her colonial mother or grandmother had had. With less physical work required to run a home, the wife was retired to a pedestal. She was expected to devote herself to providing moral uplift and comfort to her husband, who was fighting for his place in the difficult outside world. She was expected to provide loving care and a moral example for her children.

Where sex was concerned, the proper lady of the 1800s was supposed to engage in it only to please her husband, as a wifely duty. Women were not supposed to have desires of their own. The whole subject of sex became taboo, hidden behind a veil of extreme modesty.

The man of the house was a much more distant figure now. He was away all day, unavailable to his family. He assumed a new authority in the home because it was his somewhat mysterious activities in the outside world that were now the family's sole source of support.

Children were spending less time at home as well. No longer could they find training or models for their adult years within the family. The future could no longer be reliably predicted. Special education was required to prepare for the new challenges of the commercial world, and the number of years that a child was thought to need schooling, as well as the hours spent in school, began to lengthen.

Only Mother remained at home, still gaining her rewards from maintaining that home for others who were now gone much of the day. In general, women had little choice but to remain at home, for there were few ways they could earn a living outside. In the middle of the nineteenth century, women still had no legal control over property, could not vote and were poorly educated.

In a country that was founded on ideas of independence and equality, it was perhaps only a matter of time before women would rebel against their dependent status. The first serious women's rights protest was held in Seneca Falls, New York, in 1848. It was a gathering that singled out three objectives: property rights, opportunity for higher education and the right to vote.

The notion of coeducation began to grow, marked by the decision of the University of Michigan to open its doors to women in 1879. Meanwhile, the factory system was presenting the first real opportunities for women to become wage earners. Though salaries and working conditions were far from ideal, for the first time it was possible for a respectable single woman to support herself.

By 1900, the American woman was standing at the crest of a wave whose ripples would shake the foundations of family life as it had existed in the past.

Life in this century has changed so enormously, and the shifts have come with such rapidity, that it is sometimes difficult to see it all in true perspective. In 1900, half of America's families still lived on a farm and many had as yet no electricity in their homes. Women still had few rights, could not vote, and though there was some unrest, most were still content with marriage and motherhood. They still attracted men with their modesty and air of helplessness.

World War I was a landmark in the transition of women's roles, taking many out of their homes for the first time to fill in for the men who had gone to war. Once liberated, many were reluctant to return to their old retiring roles. In 1920, women were given the right to vote, a visible symbol of their changing status.

Another outward sign of the changes that were taking place could be seen in what women were wearing. The layers of clothing began to dwindle. Sleeves and hemlines became shorter. Then the 1920s brought us the flapper, whose short skirts and boyish hair bobs were unlike any woman's look in the history of the sexes. Skirts have gone up and down since, with the fashion, but never again have women been willing to hide themselves or bind themselves in as they had done for so many centuries.

Once women were out in the world, it was inevitable that courtship styles would change. For the first time there were public amusements such as movies, sports events and dances where young people could get acquainted free from the watchful eye of chaperones. It became possible to get to know a variety of prospective marriage partners who had no connection to family ties. Romantic attraction began to replace family considerations in the choice of a mate.

As men and women mingled more freely, sex also began to acquire a different meaning in a relationship. The automobile brought new privacy; spooning on the porch gave way to petting in the back seat. There was more opportunity for sex and, with the improvement of contraceptive devices in the late 1950s, less danger of pregnancy. Increasingly, women no longer expected to endure sex as a wifely duty, but began to feel entitled to enjoy it and gain their own satisfactions from it. Throughout society, there was a general relaxing of the old puritan attitudes about sex, an open acceptance of the new mores.

The idea of sexual compatability became an important factor in marital happiness. Achieving orgasm became the prime topic of books and articles for women. Manuals appeared in profusion and sex therapy emerged as a new kind of profession. Perhaps, as some believe, this is a healthy reaction against the artificial taboos and guilt feelings associated with sex in the past. But it placed a new burden on marriage, a new pressure on men and women to learn to perform better in bed.

As marriages were becoming more dependent on personal attraction and physical gratification, families were losing more of their old practical functions. Children spent more time in school and in organized recreation. Medical care and the protection of the aged passed on to specialists. Cooking, cleaning and laundering became easier and more mechanized every day. What was left for the homemaker to do at home?

The answer was to care for young children and, just as had been true in the past, to give love, companionship and moral support to husbands. Both are admirable goals, but not necessarily full-time occupations, particularly once children spend most of the day in school. For many women, lack of other purposes was leading to an excessive involvement in their children's lives, leading to dependent children *and* dependent mothers—mothers who found themselves without focus in their lives once their children no longer needed them.

As society became overwhelmingly urban rather than rural, family size continued to shrink to meet the limitations of available housing and rising costs of raising a family. Women were planning their pregnancies closer together. Medical advances were giving them more years to look forward to when they were still healthy and active and without major child-rearing responsibilities. The need to find new outlets became more pressing. By the time *The Feminine Mystique* came along in the 1960s, it fell on fertile ground. It was no wonder that women were feeling a "vague malaise" about their lives. Many of them just didn't have enough meaningful work to do.

The steady emergence of the dollar as a measure of the worth of one's efforts emphasized the housewife's dilemma. The nature and meaning of work had changed drastically over the years. No longer a necessity for sheer physical survival, work was also becoming less meaningful as a source of personal satisfaction. The skilled craftsman was giving way to the machine. Small businessmen found it harder to compete with chain-store operations. Workers were becoming more anonymous. It was difficult to see the results of a day's labor any longer except in terms of money. So work that paid poorly was not highly valued. Housework, once considered an honorable task, was losing its status because it was unpaid labor.

There was another good reason why the paycheck assumed greater importance in people's lives. The modern conveniences we have come to consider necessities are expensive, and our wants have grown. Improved working conditions have given us more leisure time—and the desire to fill it with recreation. Tennis rackets, skis, boats and campers have become standard equipment for many American families. With the growth of the suburbs, two-car families have become commonplace. It would be hard to find families today who do not want to own television sets, washing machines and dryers.

At the same time, inflation has eaten away at family buying power. Owning a home, still so integral a part of the American dream, has become almost out of reach for many families. The median price of a new home in 1976 was $40,000, up from $21,000 just ten years before, and interest rates have moved into unprecedented double digits. An average-size family car can cost $6,000 today, and the price for gasoline, as well as for automobile insurance, has more than doubled since the start of the 1970s. The energy crisis has escalated heating bills. Food, clothing and medical expenses have followed the inflationary spiral. College tuitions have increased at a frightening rate. A diploma that cost $1,600 for grandfather had gone up to $16,000 for mothers and dads of today. Before many of today's children reach college, there are signs that the price tag will have doubled again. Even successful fathers find it hard to meet this kind of burden. With the family's financial needs growing and responsibilities at home shrinking, there was every good reason for more women to enter the work force. And they have done so, in numbers that exceeded anyone's predictions. Between 1940 and 1973, participation by women in the labor force increased 68 percent.[3] A national survey by the Institute of Life Insurance found that only about one in four young women intended to spend little or no time working during her lifetime.[4] Increased earning power has given added impetus to the equality women were already achieving at home. But while homemaking was not enough to require full-time attention from most women, leaving home did produce a new kind of problem for American families. If mother is not at home, who will mind the children?

Compared with families of the past, today's family has lost most of its practical functions. Once a productive unit that manufactured its own food, clothing, tools, furniture and shelter, the family today purchases all of these things from others. Protection has been taken over by the police, the courts, the insurance companies. We buy tickets for much of our recreation today and bring outside amusement into our homes via television. Religious functions have been given to the church, education to the schools. TV dinners and no-iron shirts have made it possible to do without many of the domestic functions of a wife. Women with job opportunities have less need for a husband to support them. Considering the changes in the world around us, the increasing expectations of our marriages and the problems of raising children, the trend toward measuring fulfillment in terms of personal success outside the home, what is most surprising may not be our rising divorce rates but the fact that the family is still with us at all.

For in spite of all the forces working against traditional marriage, more people than ever are choosing to marry, and the majority of them still want to have children. While we may have found other sources for our practical needs, no one has yet devised a successful alternative method of providing for our deeper needs for emotional security. There is still reward in commitment to others, still satisfaction in bringing up children to take their place in life that cannot be compensated for with professional achievements.

The family has retained one basic function that has sustained it over the centuries. It remains the one place where we can hope for lifetime unconditional acceptance, no matter how many changes occur outside. No one has yet devised a better way to serve our fundamental human needs for emotional security, the preparation of children for responsible adulthood and a framework that gives meaning and happiness to life.

But the forces that have caused fear for the family's future have become stronger in the past decade. And with this increase has come a crisis of confidence. The more we read and hear about how much we have changed, the more we doubt many of our old values—even though most of us still believe in them.

Let's move from the past to see how the families of the present are living and coping with today's challenges.

III

New Roles for Mother and Father

MOTHERS AT WORK

People were furious for one of two reasons. One group said, "The questionnaire makes me feel I'm just a housewife in New Jersey and everyone else is doing cancer research and there's something wrong with me because I have a house and children." The other group said, "The questionnaire makes me feel there's something wrong with me because I don't have children and I'm not living in the suburbs."[5]

It is a complicated time to be a woman. And mothers are feeling the strain, at home and at work, of trying to redefine their roles in today's world.

It was a lot simpler when the proper path seemed clear-cut. Motherhood was the accepted goal—and anyone could give a description of a "good mother": warm, supportive, patient. A good cook and housekeeper. Someone who was always there, who knew almost before you did when you were not feeling well, who always sensed what was needed, whether the need was to fix a broken toy, settle a fight or make a bruise feel better. Mothers were supposed to devote their lives to making everyone else feel better—and to get their own satisfactions from their unselfishness.

They wrote songs about that kind of Mom ... and young men grew up wanting to find a girl "just like the girl who married dear old Dad."

But along the way, something happened. Women's lib came along and told Mom she was trapped, shut away in the house all day with those kids. Spiraling inflation made her feel that she might be doing more for the family by going out to work than staying at home. And everyone seemed to decide that women could find more fulfilling things to do with their lives than remain in their traditional roles as housekeepers and nurturers.

So in millions of homes today, when Father arrives home from work, Mother may be coming up the walk right behind him. The practical problems that these two-paycheck families must solve are many. But even more difficult to cope with are some of the inner difficulties that almost invariably come with doing away with tradition.

In spite of the growing numbers of working mothers today, women are still struggling to accept this pattern. After all, the division of male-female roles and functions have been part of our heritage for all of recorded time. We don't disturb deep-rooted concepts so easily or so quickly as statistics of change might lead us to believe. For the first time, more than half the mothers of school-age children in America are working—but that old picture of the nurturing, ever-available mother often remains in their heads. And even the most "liberated" of mothers may find herself trying to live up to two sets of expectations, the old and the new. Many find that juggling two roles is not as easy as they had been led to believe. Even a seemingly sympathetic husband is not enough to ease the strain, for husbands, too, are subject to that old notion of a mother's proper role.

Kathy Molcano, an assistant producer at a TV station, is typical of many working mothers when she says:

> My husband has been great in lots of ways. He doesn't mind pitching in with the house or helping with the kids. But there's no question that he is *helping*, that I am the one who remains responsible. I don't have to stay at home with them myself, but it is my responsibility to find a replacement for myself. If someone gets sick, child or sitter, that's my problem. If someone gets up in the middle of the night, guess who takes care of them? He's really saying, "If you want to work that's great, but you're still the mother in this house. It's still your job to see to the children."
>
> And I have to confess, in my heart I feel that's true. I'm the one who *should* be responsible for

those kids. I'm their mother. As a result I feel
pressured most of the time. I want to do justice to
both my kids and my job, and as a result I
sometimes feel I'm not doing right by either.

In spite of changing roles and aspirations, and a
supportive husband, Kathy remains, like most
mothers today, what Jean Curtis calls "the psychological parent." In her book, *Working Mothers*, Ms.
Curtis describes this parent as the one who "always
has a direct personal responsibility for the where-
abouts and the feelings of each child ... Who knows
what's happening inside the head of the child all
the time? Who knows what emotional supports
they need, what size shoes they wear, what diseases
they've been exposed to, who their teachers are,
what kind of work the first grade does, who their
friends are, how the baby lies—on his stomach or
back ... ?"[6]

In almost every case the answer remains the
mother, even when she has a demanding career. So
working mothers carry a double burden, and because it is so much a part of our image of what
motherhood is supposed to mean, they actually are
loath to give it up.

Not only is child care considered the mother's
responsibility, but an amazing number of working
mothers still consider housework as their rightful
duty as well. Women have for so long gained their
basic identities from being the hub of household
activity, that they often find they cannot give up this
role easily. Even career success does not compen-

sate if they feel they are not also fulfilling their first line of duty at home. They may complain about lack of help from husbands and children, but in reality they don't want it. Sometimes they don't even want hired help. They prefer to perform two jobs because relinquishing their housework produces too much guilt.

Dr. Alexandra Symonds, past president of the American Association for the Advancement of Psychoanalysis, noted in an interview that women like this have "the feeling that they have to prove their femininity by overcompensating in their roles as wife and mother." She cited several studies as examples, including a survey of doctors which showed that women psychiatrists had more children than their male counterparts, and another which revealed that 87 percent of the female doctors questioned did their own housework, despite their full-time professional commitments.[7]

Often women are not aware how deep their feelings go about their place in the home until they try to leave. Says Joan Hayes, an articulate and obviously intelligent woman in her forties: I never had a doubt that I should be more than just a wife and mother. I've been strongly affected by the times and my many working friends. I enrolled in school part time as soon as the youngest of my children entered school, but just a course or two at a time so that no one would be affected at home. By the time I had my social work degree my oldest son was in college, my daughter in high school and my youngest was ten. I thought it would be a breeze to work. But the reality of a full-time job was something I had not anticipated. I have no more free time. I feel rushed all the time. I seem to leave things undone in the morning and come home tired to start dinner at night.

Stan, my husband, was very helpful when I was in school and even more when I took the job. He would have pitched in willingly. But my feelings amazed me. When I saw him emptying the dishwasher one morning, I actually felt angry. That was *my* job. I didn't want anyone else to fill my place at home.

It wasn't until I began working that I was aware just how much my home life is truly my first priority. It isn't that my work is not meaningful to me. It's more than a hobby. But I don't want to become head of the agency. I don't want to stay around talking cases after work. I want to do my job, do it well—then leave promptly at 5 o'clock to come home to my family.

In fact, I really want to leave before 5 o'clock. I think I started a full-time job too soon. I feel that the quality of our home life was much better when I was here seeing that things ran smoothly. I know I was much more in touch with the kids.

When the women's movement began to challenge women to seek more from life than a single role as homemaker, there was almost a conspiracy of silence about the personal adjustments involved in combining a job with family life. The women we read about were "wonder women" who came home calm and collected to whip up jiffy gourmet meals and alternately minister to needs of children and husband during the evening.

"I am woman," was the cry. "I can do it all."

Finally—fortunately—we are realizing the truth: No one can do it all. If a mother is to accept a major commitment outside of her home without wearing herself out in the process, her own priorities must change, and her family's living patterns must change as well. Women who seem to have made this transition most successfully have advice to offer for those who are struggling to balance their double lives more equitably. And the most crucial change that seems to be necessary is a personal one, a re-examination of what it means to be a woman, wife and mother today.

Working necessarily must mean relinquishing some of the psychological rewards women have enjoyed for their excellence at the traditional female roles of cooking, cleaning and child care. Only a more realistic evaluation of the importance of these rewards can put a changed life focus into proper perspective.

"Look at what you have to offer to your kids as a stay-at-home mother compared to a mother who is involved in the wider world," one working mother suggests. "Isn't it likely that your personal growth will ultimately aid their growth? That you are ensuring a better relationship later on because you will be able to communicate better on their level? Your most important function in your home should not be as a housekeeper. Nor is your physical presence going to solve all of your children's problems in growing up. If you can give up the ego thing that comes with feeling like the indispensable mommy at home, you may be able to see that you are doing more for your kids by allowing them to be more flexible and independent."

"You can't work out new patterns until you can recognize and believe that your own needs are as valid as those of the rest of the family," another mother advises. It's hard for women to see themselves outside the context of the family. But it is really only the mother who has ever been expected to build a life around other people's needs. That's not a valid basis for a life. Husbands have always had both work and family in their lives. Children are occupied in their growing up years with learning how to function when they leave the family. While you want to give them the love and concern and encouragement they need, they don't need your entire being. It's absolutely necessary that you make your family understand that your personal needs are important, too."

Dr. Nancy D. Stevens, director of career counseling at Hunter College, has for a number of years conducted seminars for mothers returning to work. She confirms the value of expressing your needs, illustrating the point with a story about a woman who had problems with her son following her return to work.

> He had been a healthy boy, but suddenly he seemed to be getting sick all the time and his mother was missing valuable days at work because

of him. It finally dawned on her that perhaps this was his way of protesting her job. So she talked with him, told him how much she missed being home when he came home from school and how much it bothered her that he might be bothered.

But she told him something else. She explained that she had been very unhappy when the boy signed up for a midget league football team, that she worried about his being hurt and hated seeing him come home from practice so exhausted. But because she had realized how much the team mattered to him, she had tried to understand, she told him. And she asked his understanding of her job in just that same way.

Her admission allowed him to talk freely about how much he missed her at home. After that, there were no more sick days. In fact, she noted a great change in his attitude, more consideration about giving her help with dinner and dishes and more interest in asking about her job. They understood each other better now, and that kind of understanding can make the transition period easier on everyone.

The demands of a growing family convince many working women that compromises must be made on the job as well as at home. "You must come to terms somewhere along the line with the limitations of your own energy," a mother of three school-age children comments. "You just have to evaluate your work in terms of your present home situation, perhaps postponing a serious push up the ladder until you can afford the time and effort that involves. Sometimes part-time work is wiser for a while. You simply cannot do everything, and you must choose what is most important to you."

Communication within the family can help to resolve many of these conflicts. Changing roles is not just a mother's problem. Everyone needs the chance to explore feelings and expectations, to understand one another's needs better. When there is understanding and good will, the practical problems brought on by a mother's outside commitments can usually be solved by new patterns that are suited to the present situation rather than to the way families used to live. The solutions seem as individual as the particular people involved. One family may decide they want to allot the budget differently so as to provide for hiring outside help. Another may prefer to set up more cooperative living patterns, dividing home responsibilities more equitably.

Teaching children to take more responsibility for their own needs is a beneficial change in either case, but again it is something that works only when a mother is able to free herself from the compulsion to do too much for her youngsters. "I had to change my perception of my kids," a mother noted. "A ten-year-old is perfectly capable of running a washing machine and dryer. I'd simply never thought to ask before. It still looks funny to me to watch him and I still feel pangs because I'm not doing it myself. But you know what? I'm proud of him—and he's proud of himself for helping."

Her husband can be a working woman's best ally, but gaining his support may require understanding the real distress many men feel at changes in their own traditional roles, something that will be discussed more fully in another chapter.

Some working mothers with common problems have found that one of the best sources for practical help can be each other. A group in a Chicago suburb sat down with their children's after-school schedules, rearranged things wherever possible so that dates like music lessons or dentist appointments could be scheduled on the same afternoon, then paid a responsible college student to serve as chauffeur. The same system works for after-school activities such as club meetings, team practices and necessary errands.

Another group has formed a telephone network that makes at least one mother available in case a child's own parents cannot be at the phone for messages after school.

In New York, six women set up a marketing cooperative. Each one does her own major shopping, but they take turns on the midweek fill-ins for milk, fruit, salad or bread. A West Coast group of mothers has a similar arrangement for pickups and deliveries at the cleaners, laundry, shoe repair shop or library. In all cases, husbands pitch in.

Free time is the greatest lack when a job is tacked onto an already busy family schedule. Time management, something that is traditionally taught in business, is equally valuable at home. Begin by determining what is most important to you, working mothers advise. Sort out which parts of your life you want to maintain, which are giving you real rewards and which are just time fillers or things you feel guilty about turning down. It's all too easy to have your precious free time whittled away. As a working mother you can't afford to help every worthy cause, accept every social invitation or even to agree to every request from your own family. You must learn to say no, to order your priorities in your free time as well as in other areas of your life if you are not to feel overwhelmed by your obligations.

Combining a work and family life and having time left over for personal relaxation is not an easy assignment—yet millions of women are doing it. A rundown of guidelines that seem to make it possible are these:

Recognize and Accept the Fact That You Can't Fill Two Jobs to Perfection at One Time
You must decide which compromises you can live with most comfortably, and these may change as your children grow. This could mean settling for part-time work or less job advancement for a time. It may mean learning to say no to unnecessary demands from your family. It definitely means admitting the limit of your human energy by not trying to fulfill every community request, every home responsibility and every job requirement to perfection. There's nothing wrong with admitting that you are human.

Learn to Recognize Your Female Hangups
The need for perfection on all fronts is nine-tenths

cultural brainwashing. We need to re-examine the meaning of being a "good" mother and wife, to realize that love, concern, encouragement and time to listen are more important than ironing or gourmet meals. Evaluate what your family needs from you on the deeper levels, not in terms of chores, and keep your sights on those goals rather than superficial tasks. And remember that the most important thing you may be able to give to your family is a positive outlook on life that comes from finding your own outside fulfillment.

Learn to Ask for Help

Martyr working mothers who insist on maintaining all the elements of their traditional full-time role at home are hurting not only themselves but their families. Your children benefit from responsibility and you may be able to build a closer relationship with your husband by working together toward a common goal. Talk it out, and with your family establish new schedules and patterns that help spread the workload around.

Try to Understand Your Husband's Point of View

Men are being asked to give up traditional support systems and take on duties that have never been part of the normal male image. It's easy to complain about lack of cooperation, but wiser to understand that your husband is struggling with old stereotypes just as you are. Time and honest talk are your best allies.

Recognize That Some of the Conflicts May Never Be Resolved

If working is a necessity, either for income or for your peace of mind, you must realize that some home satisfactions must be sacrificed. Do some careful choosing so that you can try to maintain those things that are most important to you and your family, then give up the rest with as much grace as you can muster. Accept it as the price that comes from a richer life texture.

Compromise is something every family must employ if they are to weather the changes of the times. It is not just a working mother who must be aware of this need. Children and fathers, too, will have to reassess their expectations at home. When families can talk these matters out and share in finding solutions that work best for all, the changes produced by losing a full-time mother may actually strengthen the family's solidarity.

MOTHERS AT HOME

It isn't just working mothers who need help in coming to terms with the changes in today's world. Mothers at home have problems of their own. With all of the difficulties working women have in juggling schedules and coping with personal guilt, they at least no longer have to defend their decisions to have a career. But in many circles it has become unfashionable to be "just a housewife." One rueful homemaker recently wrote a letter to *The*

New York Times asking if she had become an "endangered species." When the women's movement won the battle that allowed women to go out to work, it left many mothers battling for the right to stay at home.

"Am I peculiar?" asks Nancy Madden, a twenty-eight-year-old mother of two. "I don't want to work. My oldest child just started to kindergarten and I still have a three-year-old at home. I don't want to miss out on these years with my children. I feel no one else would care for them with the same kind of love that I do. I'm not bored and I'm not lonely. And the kids are not my only interest in life.

"Yet my own husband seems to wonder why I'm not like all those women he reads about or meets at the office. He gets after me when I call myself Mrs. Arthur Madden instead of by my own name. He asks me whether I don't want to think about a part-time job, something to keep me in touch with the world."

Nancy is feeling outside the mainstream in her decision to stay at home, but she is far from alone. Sixty million homemakers are continuing to follow the traditional woman's path. They feel comfortable there, maintaining that their choice is best for their children. Nor do they feel that they are passive and dependent because they are financially supported by their husbands. For them the old bargain holds true even in a changed world. They feel that their contributions at home are an equal share of the family load, so long as finances are adequate. Furthermore, they voice something that most observers of women's needs tend to overlook: They *like* taking care of their children.

Yet we hear little about these millions of women. The media are seriously biased in favor of what is new and tend to ignore the status quo. A woman in our community who petitioned to become the city's first lady garbage collector recently made the front page of the newspaper. The many who remain content at home are not recorded in print.

So stay-at-home mothers have been made uneasy. They are being challenged to reassess the wisdom of their ways, warned about the years ahead when their children will no longer need them, cautioned about the perils of possible divorce or widowhood when they may need to be self-supporting. Many feel out of touch with the times, unsure about their choice.

A number of women who had intended to combine careers with motherhood are surprised to find after the birth of a child that their maternal feelings are stronger than they had expected, and that juggling roles does not come easily to them. Yet even when there is no financial pressure, there is societal pressure that makes them hesitate to follow their instincts.

Lisa Taylor, a commercial artist and mother of a two-year-old daughter, sums it up well when she talks about her difficulty in deciding to stay at home:

Up to now I had always considered myself relatively well educated, kind of feisty and independent, very little influenced by what other people said or thought. I made it on my own, stayed single until I was twenty-seven, waited another six years before I had a child. Then I switched to free-lance work, feeling that I was fortunate to be able to have it both ways, stay home and breast-feed my baby like I was told good mothers should do, and still be able to have my career at home. First of all, I really didn't like breast-feeding, but I kept it up because I thought something must be wrong with me if I didn't. Second, I found I was pressured all the time, so tired that I was always depressed. I had deadlines all the time, was constantly pulled between the baby and getting my work done.

It's taken me two years to finally figure out that I'd been brainwashed. I'm a victim of propaganda. I couldn't think of giving up working because I was contemptuous of women who did that. No independent, modern, intelligent woman would stay at home to stagnate tending to a little baby, right? When I found that work and mothering weren't as easy to combine as I'd thought, I was absolutely overcome with guilt because I wasn't doing what I was told everyone else was doing with ease. It is a more difficult decision than anyone tells you. Before a woman decides to try to do everything at once, she has to take into consideration her own emotional state, her patience, the availability of help. I was listening to what everyone else said and I was totally out of touch with my own self and what is right for me. I was being suckered by women's lib.

Not all women feel the same need to work. In fact, the majority of women really would prefer to stay at home when their children are small, combining employment with homemaking during the rest of their adult careers, according to a survey conducted for the National Commission on Observance of International Women's Year.[8]

Among the most contented stay-at-home mothers are those who are following this path, taking time off when they feel they are needed at home and planning for careers later on. Some say it is unfair to ask this kind of compromise of women and not of men, but women who have relished the real satisfactions of motherhood will tell you that those who can have some of both worlds may just be the luckiest people of all.

• Life in Stages

Camille DeRosa is a woman who expresses fulfillment in both areas of her life, work and family. She left a secretarial job to stay at home when her first child was born, and remained at home to have another child. When the youngsters were ages two and four, Camille returned to school on a very limited schedule, taking a course or two each term toward a degree that would qualify her for the field of her interest, vocational counseling.

"Even that much," she says, "would not have been possible without the support of my husband, who was willing to feed the children and put them to bed while I went to classes. Ten years ago I went to work half-time, so that I could be home when the

38

children returned from school. It is only two years ago, with the kids at sixteen and fourteen, that I took a full time job. Yet I'm only forty. Don't smile when I say that. I have twenty-five years left at this job, and every chance in the world still to move ahead."

Camille's story sounds much like that of Joan Hayes, who found the realities of working more than she could handle. But there is a crucial difference. In Camille's case, the whole family assumed responsibility for seeing her through her life stages.

We knew from the start, my husband, my children and I, that I was going to be here when I was needed, but that everyone else was going to be responsible for helping me when I needed it as well. I'm not going to tell you we never have difficult days. Even at this age, occasionally the kids resent my being gone all day. But all along I brought them up to help at home, so that before I left full-time they had become responsible for a lot in the house.

I feel I fulfilled my obligation to them when I was really needed when they were younger, so I don't have the kind of guilt I might have if I had worked all along. I don't feel I have anything to make up to them. They're so busy themselves, they often aren't home before I am anyway. And they grew up knowing I expected support from them in my ambitions just the way I gave them support in theirs. They seem to respect that, even if they sometimes complain about chores.

My husband always was aware that I wanted to do something outside. He's not what you would call liberated in the sense of doing laundry, but he was willing to do what was necessary to allow me to do my thing along the way. I wouldn't take on more than I could handle with the kind of assistance he was able and willing to give. I can't speak for all families, but in our case I believe we've been able to adjust along the way because I knew I had to adjust to the realities of the different things I wanted out of life. I don't feel cheated of anything. It's a great time to be a woman. I feel my life is just beginning again. You really can have two rewarding lives today, if you can just plan it gradually.

For women who have the foresight to think of life in terms of stages, some of the conflicts of the day are eased. Camille DeRosa feels comfortable about her choices because she kept the old-fashioned commitments she felt were due to her family. In her case that meant postponing, but never abandoning, her own career.

Younger women today are seeking a different way to accomplish the same goal. Many spectators look at the rising number of childless women in their twenties with dismay, fearing for the future of the family. But a good many of these women are extremely traditional in their ultimate goals. They are simply putting their priorities in a different time sequence. They are establishing their careers first, then planning to have a family. And many speak of wanting to limit their families to a size that can be managed more easily.

Patty Hughes, thirty-one-year-old publicity director for a New York publishing company, says, "I needed to prove something to myself. I needed to know that I had what it takes to make it in the business world. Accomplishing that has done something for my feelings about myself that I can't even put into words. Now, having passed age thirty, I can think about another need, having a child. When I do, I want to be able to stay at home at least in the early years. I feel I've established my credentials now and can stay in touch through free-lance work. Even if I don't, I think I've come far enough so that I can always come back."

Lee Milton, twenty-six-year-old manager of a chain of dress shops in a southern town, voices similar sentiments for different reasons. "I wanted to work long enough to provide the money for us to have a baby without such financial sacrifice. With both of us working, we've saved enough to buy a home and are working on furnishing it. When we've gotten everything ready and have a little put away in savings, I'll be ready to give mothering my whole attention for a while."

The satisfactions of delayed parenthood seem strong among those who are adopting this relatively new trend. "I was thirty-two when my son was born," says the former editor of a woman's magazine. "I had done everything I wanted to do, been everywhere I wanted to go—for a while, at least. I was ready to stay at home and enjoy it instead of resent it. If I had had the baby at twenty-two, I think I would have been miserable at home."

"We need to realize that there are many different valid life paths today," says Carol Feit Lane, coordinator of WATCH (Women Advancing Through Career Help), a program for women seeking career guidance, at the New York University School of Continuing Education. She sees many women who are weighing a decision between home and career. "Women still have a dual commitment," Ms. Lane observes. "They need to understand that years at home are not wasted, that no decision need be a permanent one."

One of the problems Ms. Lane sees—and one mentioned by many women, particularly young mothers who have opted to stay at home—is the lack of opportunity to talk to other women who share similar concerns.

"I desperately need to find other young mothers like me to talk to," Lisa Taylor pleads. "Some of the things I used to make fun of—the women who sit around drinking coffee while the kids are playing—are things that are meaningful at certain stages of your life. I didn't know much about being a mother. I'd like to be able to find out how other mothers handle things. Most of all, I need reassurance that I'm not alone, that I'm not lazy or crazy or a traitor to womankind for doing what I feel is right for me."

The kind of reassurance Lisa is seeking used to come naturally in the neighborhood, but today's mobile and fast-paced society seems to require more formal kinds of meeting places. As a result, new kinds of groups are forming. Some are local, such as the Family Life Workshops that are detailed later in the book. Others are national in scope. The Martha Movement, founded in May 1976, is an organization that purports to give a voice to 70 million American women who identify themselves—often defensively—as homemakers. Its founder, Jinx Meila, expressed the feelings of many women when she said, "The wrong people are often speaking for the American woman, people like sociologists, economists and writers. We homemakers are always being talked to. Our opinions are never asked."[9]

Many women who firmly support equal opportunity for women in the workplace do not want to join their ranks. Instead, they want equal opportunity to stay at home to do justice to the needs of their families without embarrassment. Most of all, they want the world to acknowledge that raising children is work, too, challenging and important work that may well be done best by parents who bring love to the task. They need to feel that there is still status in listing "homemaker" as an occupation. By speaking out together these women are just beginning to make an impact of their own.

For those who continue to feel uneasy about their choice to stay at home, here is a consensus of advice from women who seem most comfortable with their decision for the family:

First and Foremost: Get in Touch With Your Own Feelings

Understand that there are no right or wrong decisions today, but a number of valid paths and the one that is right for you is the one that gives you

43

greatest peace of mind. At this point in our development as a more equal male-female society, it remains true that mothers continue to feel a greater sense of obligation to the personal care of their children than do fathers. It has yet to be proven that this instinct is not the right one. If your feelings about your role as a mother are strong enough to give you serious qualms about working at an outside job, go with your feelings. Regardless of what other people are doing, this is the right decision for you.

Realize That Your Decisions Are Not Necessarily for a Lifetime

Your needs change over the years and so do those of your family. Child rearing is not a lifelong occupation and can be combined with preparation for resumption of outside commitments as home demands lessen. You need not feel that you are precluding a career by giving priority to your family during one phase of your life.

Use the Years at Home to Grow as a Person

Take advantage of this period to explore your future personal goals, to try your talents in different directions, to read and pursue new interests, to investigate future career options. If you maintain the feeling that you are expanding your horizons and becoming a more interesting person, you'll feel no need to apologize for being at home. Your working friends may envy you.

Discuss Your Feelings With Your Family

As is true with working women, the most satisfied mothers at home are those whose decision has the support of their husbands (and children who are old enough to understand). Let your family know that you need their reassurance. But even though you are at home, make them understand that your needs are important, too. Raise your children and encourage your husband to share responsibilities in preparation for the time when you are ready for outside commitments. When your family is involved in your goals and can help you find time to prepare for a broader life eventually, they may be as proud as you are when the day comes for you to "leave home."

Find Others Who Share Your Dilemmas—and Your Values

Whenever social customs undergo a major change, whether concerned with something as serious as rights for women or as frivolous as long hair for men, there is normally a surge at the start, then a leveling off to a saner norm. While more women are working, more are also beginning to evaluate just how much of their mothering role they are willing to give up. Women who feel that they are going counter to a trend need reassurance in their values. One of the best ways to find it is to reach out to one another, to reinforce together the values of family commitment.

45

With the growing knowledge that millions do share this preference, that there is no one right direction for all and, most of all, that there are enough patterns and options to allow for many kinds of satisfactions in life, more women may feel relieved of the pressure of making either/or decisions. They will be able to stay at home to enjoy their children if this is their present choice, planning for future choices that will truly make it possible to give life a second focus later on.

THE NEW FATHER

Women who are having difficulty redefining their roles in today's world are not alone. Women's liberation, with its questioning of traditional values, is having an inevitable effect on men, one that can be even more complex since society so far has had far less sympathy for the dilemmas of husbands and fathers in a changing world.

Their problems are real, for men have grown up with their own stereotypes about what it means to be a "good" husband and father. Once that was equated with being a good provider and a strong head of the house. We still expect men to go out and succeed in the world, but that's no longer enough. Wives are asking that their husbands become more sensitive to the emotional needs of the family. Men are expected to be companions, partners and friends as well as breadwinners. They are asked to remain the stronger sex, yet to give their wives equal say in family decisions, to impose discipline and set standards and at the same time to be pals to their children. Wives who used to submit dutifully to their husbands in bed now expect tenderness, technique—and orgasms.

It's no wonder men are uneasy about living up to all of these expanded expectations—and in many cases a working wife only compounds the problem.

Even the best-intentioned husband, one who firmly believes that his wife has the right to pursue the satisfactions of an outside career, seldom has envisioned this in terms of *his* having to do the laundry as a result. And even when he is willing to do the laundry, many a male remains embarrassed at having anyone outside the house know about it, because society has been slow to change its verdict about which jobs are properly "women's work."

It's conditioning, not male chauvinism, that is at work here. And the same kind of conditioning can cause negative psychological reactions on a deeper level. Losing the role of sole provider can diminish the feeling of manhood for those who were brought up to define themselves in these terms. A man can feel threatened by a wife who becomes better educated or more successful than he, may fear that his wife will no longer look up to him in the same way once he is no longer her major link to the outside world. If the marriage has been less than ideal, he may worry about his wife's new financial independence or the new men she will meet on the job. And he will likely encounter

47

requests for new participation in household duties that have never been part of the masculine image.

Wives who can understand the underlying reasons that men find these developments so threatening can do much to help alleviate the situation by offering needed reassurance of continued love and respect, rather than anger at a husband's seeming unwillingness to change. When a wife expresses to her husband how important he remains to her, how much she continues to need his moral support, it makes it much easier for him to feel supportive.

Some women find that their husbands respond far more positively when they are involved in planning for new routines and solutions, when they are asked for help and made to feel equally responsible for seeing that the household continues to run smoothly. "My husband was much happier about things after I asked him to help me screen baby-sitters for the children," one mother relates. "I realized that he was concerned and I think having some say about how things would be done in my absence made him easier in his mind about the kids."

Another mother observes, "In spite of his qualms about it, when we sat down as a family to find ways to get the house better organized, it was my husband who really took charge and found ways to make it work. Then he felt very good about the whole thing."

• Seeing the Benefits

Ultimately, the most important thing that will enable men to accept changes in their accustomed roles is their realization of the negative effects of the traditional definitions of masculinity we have been living with, advises Stephen Dworkin, a clinical social worker who has initiated a course called "Changing Roles for Men" at Southern Connecticut State College.

As Dworkin points out,

> We've put an intolerable burden on men all these years, the entire economic burden of supporting a family, plus the old stereotypes that a man must not show weakness or admit to problems, must never reveal his emotions. These notions have kept men from really sharing in their marriage relationships or from becoming emotionally close to their children.
>
> While women were allowed to identify themselves only as wives and mothers, cutting them off from the rest of the world, men, conversely, have been allowed to assume their identity only from work. Restricting of their role has made it impossible for men to take an active part in child rearing or home management without running into negative reactions and feelings. That's why when women began moving into the working world—men's turf—so many men found it a threat. It's because women are freer to do both things today that men are able to have new options as well.

49

But many men are not sufficiently aware still of just how severe are the problems that society has given them. They must unlearn their old self-images and become open to new possibilities. As men begin to understand the personal benefits from sharing roles, they will be able to accept changes for themselves as well as for women. We need time to begin to see the rewards.

Like women who need new role models for changing life patterns, men can benefit greatly from meeting others who are going through the same kinds of value transitions. Though male conditioning makes it more difficult for men to seek out group support, the need has developed a small "men's movement," a complementary effect of the women's movement. It began with divorced men who were forced to reassess their roles because of a life crisis, according to Stephen Dworkin, but has grown into larger numbers of "consciousness-raising" groups trying to sort out what masculinity should mean today. Men are holding national conferences to talk about their changing roles and a Men's Resource Center in Portland, Oregon, now publishes a national newsletter.

"The next step I'd like to see," says Dworkin, "is putting discussions like these in the form of forums where men and women could attend and explore their options together."

Without benefit of an official forum, men could better understand some of the compensations of a working wife and a changed life-style simply by talking more openly to one another, for there are many husbands who have discovered rewards that far outweigh any new demands on them.

"Since my wife went to work," one man reports, "she has new understanding of the stresses I have on the job every day. She's far more understanding. We have more in common. And while I can't say I love helping with the housework, I do recognize that I have a more stimulating woman to talk to these days."

"My wife's job has liberated *me*," another pleased husband observes. "For eight hours a day, five days a week, I've worked at a job I didn't like in order to provide for my family. Several years ago when my wife decided to go back to school to get a degree as a librarian, I was a little resentful that she could do what she wanted while I was trapped. Then it occurred to me that if she were working, I could afford to make a change, too. I've begun taking education courses at night and plan to go into teaching when I'm qualified. I'll be able to take longer vacations, spend more time with the kids before they are all gone, and most important— because I have a working wife—I have the chance to escape a rut I thought I was stuck in for the rest of my life."

For many men, the richest rewards of all have resulted from spending more time with their children. David Bartlett is one of a number of young fathers who has chosen to cut back to part-time work in order to help care for his newborn child.

"This experience has totally changed my feelings," he declares. "I know my daughter in an intimate way that would never had been possible if I had only been home at night after she was asleep. I feel much closer to my wife, understand her problems at home better, and she is grateful to me because this arrangement has allowed her to continue to work part-time, too. I do have career ambitions and eventually will return to a regular work schedule. I consider this as a temporary phase in my life—one that has enriched me and greatly strengthened my bond to my wife and my child."

This kind of shared parenting remains an exception, but even fathers who have difficulty accepting other kinds of role changes seem to agree that closer relationships with their children are worth working for. Often this has been accomplished within the confines of a traditional lifestyle. From those who feel they have succeeded in finding small ways to make large improvements, here are a few suggestions for improving father-child relations:

Be a Father, Not a Pal

Busy fathers tend to think of time with children in terms of tossing a ball, going on an outing or playing a game. It's fine to play games, but remember that while youngsters have many playmates in their lives, they have only one father. What matters more than play is time for talk, private and serious talk, something that is often best accomplished in quiet times together—on a walk, doing errands or working together on projects around the house. Look for opportunities for this kind of natural, companionable time with your children in your normal routines at home.

Set Aside Private Time for Each Child

It doesn't take hours together to develop meaningful communication. It does take your undivided attention. Show your special interest in each child's world—and introduce him or her to yours. Take the children to see where you work and go with them to see their schools, playgrounds and favorite spots. Give your children more of a sense of your world away from home, what your days are like, and try to get that same kind of feeling from them. Get to know each other better; get involved.

Learn to Level With Your Children

All parents tend to feel guilty, but fathers most of all tend not to discuss important questions with their children. When children sense that they are excluded from your important concerns, they are less likely to feel free to confide in you. Discussions need not be the kind to worry a child (such as how to pay the rent), but sharing your feelings about your way of life, your values, your friends, your hopes for the future help your children to know you better and encourage them to share their confidences with you in return.

Become Involved in the Daily Care of Your Child

Fathers who will make the effort to share in the day-to-day activities that are part of a child's life, who are part-time supervisors of meals, baths, bedtime, dressing, shopping—whatever activities their work schedules will allow—report that they just naturally become involved as well in the kind of teaching, correcting, comforting and loving that are the most important elements in a close parent-child relationship.

"I've benefited enormously from making the effort to become a more equal partner where child care is concerned," says one father, "and just as important, I think my children will grow up without the same kinds of rigid stereotypes I had about what is a father's proper role."

Ideas about that "proper role" are likely to change even more. When the Nurtury, the nation's first nursery school with a predominantly male staff, opened its doors in Sherman Oaks, California, it was expected that most applicants would be divorced mothers happy at the opportunity to give their children contact with male figures. What happened in fact is that half of the children enrolled came from two-parent families. These children see the men at school make lunch and wash the dishes afterwards, something many youngsters have never seen in their own homes. And what the children like best of all, according to founder Steve Brody, is the idea that they can climb into a man's lap and be cuddled. A generation of children who grow up considering this a normal role for men is bound to do things differently at home when they are parents.

A recent *New York Times*-CBS poll shows that 48 percent of those questioned believed that the most satisfying marriage is one in which husband and wife both have jobs, both do housework and both take care of the children. There was marked preference in the 18-to-29-year-old group, which opted for this life-style by almost three to one.[10]

Right now many families continue to struggle to change the attitudes that stand in the way of a more equal sharing of life's roles between the sexes. If this kind of sharing is to become a reality, however, it is more than attitudes that must change. Our working world is not set up to allow easily for time off for family life—not for mothers, even less for fathers.

Yet there are ways, and the beginnings of change can be seen right now in experiments that seem to benefit employers as much as their employees. Any look at today's family has to include mothers and fathers at work as well as at home—for one life inevitably affects the other.

IV

Working Parents

When President Jimmy Carter took office in 1976, one of his first memos to top White House staffers read, "I want you to spend an adequate amount of time with your husbands, wives and children. We are going to be here a long time and all of you will be more valuable to me and the country with rest and a stable home life."

The President was acknowledging a long-standing problem: how to combine the demands of work with commitment to family life. In a country where the work ethic is so strong, where moving ahead and making more money has been the driving force for so long, the idea that work should be moderated to make more time for family is slow to come.

More women want to work—but they want to work less during the years when their children are young. The idea of spending more time with growing children is appealing to more men. Traditionally, it has been almost impossible to give anything other than a nine-to-five day and have a meaningful occupation. But at last there are some hopeful signs of change.

For example: No one stirs when James Porter reports to work at 10 A.M., after dropping his son off at nursery school. Nor is anyone upset when Carolyn Wright takes off at 3 P.M. to be at home with her school-age children. Both these parents are employees of companies on "flextime," a plan that allows workers to choose their own hours. The total workday remains the normal seven or eight hours, but there is only a four- to five-hour core period when all employees must be present. Each worker is free to elect the starting and stopping time that fits best with his or her personal needs.

Most commonly, core hours are between 10 A.M. and 3 P.M. For a couple with school-age children, this could mean that by balancing their work shifts, one parent can always be at home when the children are home. One parent might choose to work from 7 A.M. to 3 P.M., leaving the other to see to breakfast and get the children off to school. The early worker can then return at 3 P.M., devote the afternoon to children and chores and have dinner ready before the other spouse returns home. Parents of preschoolers would need a sitter for fewer hours and could spend more time with their young children.

Flextime may not solve the problem of who will do the housework but it does make the division of labor easier. More important, it shifts the day's scheduling to allow parents more time with their children.

For Joyce and Dan Atkins, parents of four children, flextime hours make the crucial difference in allowing them to be on hand when they need to be. Mrs. Atkins is able to leave work early any day when her children need her for rides or trips to the dentist, or when they want her to attend a special after-school event. If one of the children is ill, the Atkins can make arrangements between them to be at home for a good portion of the day. "Before flextime I'd usually call in sick if I had to take one of the kids someplace or had to do something else," Mrs. Atkins says. "Now I'll stay out and do my errands but make up the time later."

Even a slight flexibility in hours can make a large difference to the family. Data clerk Rita Gomez used to report to her job at a New York insurance company at 8:25 A.M. It was extremely difficult for her to get her one-year-old son up and out to a sitter in time for her to get to work on time. "My husband is gone by seven thirty A.M. so he can't help me in the morning," she says. "I have to get my son dressed and take him by bus to the sitter's home. I used to be late to work all the time. I used to say awake at night worrying if I was going to be late again and get fired. Since flextime my starting time is nine A.M. It makes all the difference, that little time. I have no more problem with the sitter who didn't like getting the baby so early. And the pressure is off. On flextime there is no such thing as late. You just make it up."

Flextime originated in Germany in the 1960s and is the accepted work style for more than one million European men and women. It began in the U.S.

with subsidiaries of overseas companies and was successful enough to be copied by many American firms. It is now estimated that 13 percent of American companies have some form of flextime, and the number is expected to increase in the years ahead.

The plan offers obvious benefits for workers. It alleviates traffic jams, allows more time for outside activities, doctor and dentist appointments, meetings or shopping. But companies benefit as well. They report improved employee morale and job satisfaction, reduced rates of turnover, drastic decreases in tardiness and very often there is increased productivity. It costs a company nothing in terms of salary or benefits—only a change in attitude that acknowledges the personal lives of employees.

Other companies are responding to the desire for more flexible working arrangements by creating more part-time work. Fifteen years ago there was only one part-timer for every ten full-time workers. Today the ratio is one to five and a half. Half of the seven million women who joined the labor force in the past decade entered as part-timers. They can be found clerking in department stores, teaching, selling insurance or standing watch as security guards. Control Data Corporation recently opened the only completely part-time operation in the world, employing women to work shifts while their children were in school, and students to fill the afternoons.

Part-time workers are usually not paid proportionate benefits for their labors, a sore point with some, but at this time many women are willing to accept this shortcoming in order to be able to combine paid work with homework more easily. A more serious problem to many is that part-time work tends to be limited to less skilled, lower-paying occupations.

A few women—and a handful of men, as well—have managed to make their own part-time niches. Each one who has done so is a role model for others who want to follow this path. Sometimes it happens almost by accident and proves to the powers that be the potential benefits in using employees who are not able or willing to work full time.

When my own children were young I was once offered a job filling in on a temporary basis while my city sought a permanent director for a newly established office. I accepted on the basis of a three-day week, working 9 A.M. to 3 P.M. The city fathers agreed because they thought it would be a short-lived arrangement. What happened instead is that both the city and I found the job could be done competently on a part-time schedule. When the scope of the position expanded, I was able to get permission to hire a qualified associate direc-tor—another working mother—to fill the two days I was not working. The city benefited from getting a diversity of skills neither of us could offer alone. It was a lesson to all concerned about the potential talents available from mothers who are not ready to leave their children full time.

There have been similar experiences in almost every field. The most illustrious example is Carol Greenwald, now Commissioner of Banks for the state of Massachusetts, who was able to convince her employers, Boston's Federal Reserve Bank, to allow her to continue as an economist part-time after she had a baby. Roxanne Conlin, the mother of two young children, was recently appointed the first half-day Assistant Attorney General in the state of Iowa. Two women in Los Altos, California, are sharing a job as an editorial assistant. A husband and wife team are sharing an appointment as professor at Hampshire College.

Job pairers are able to offer some special benefits to their employers. They can double up during peak work periods or fill in for each other during times of sickness or vacation. Pilot programs are going on in California, Maryland and Massachusetts that could eventually open up 5 to 10 percent of all state jobs for flexible schedules and shared work. In Palo Alto right now, employees are sharing positions as diverse as librarians, parking monitors and personnel administrators. In the San Francisco Bay area, some 120 teachers were rescued from layoffs by sharing their jobs.

As the potential benefits of paired jobs become better known, the search for them will become easier. Right now it remains the task of the individual to find a compatible partner and then convince employers that they will benefit by hiring two for the price of one. Knowing that it is succeeding elsewhere will help in the search. Two young mothers in Greenwich, Connecticut, conducted their job hunt by talking the local newspaper into doing a feature story about them. Once hired, they alternated baby-sitting for each other to make the plan work out easily at home.

Here and there a company pioneers in creating opportunities for women with families. Perhaps the most striking example is the Connecticut Savings Bank. Several years ago Paul Johnson, the president, decided that his personnel problems might well be solved if he could attract the community's bright, well-educated mothers to his bank. "These women are our most underutilized resource," Johnson says. "It's a fallacy that every employee must work from eight-thirty to four-thirty. We have peak hours that can easily be covered during school hours. We let women work while their children are in school; we'll even fill in for them during school vacations. This kind of plan works most easily in lower-level positions, but we've learned that it can work in management, too. Some of our mothers have been promoted to become officers of the bank—part time. We now have a lending officer, corporate secretary, customer relations officer and a student loan officer, all mothers who work around their home responsibilities."

Initially, Johnson reports, his personnel department protested vigorously at the extra scheduling work involved in this plan. "But the caliber of woman we attract has more than made up for the trouble. We've made a quantum leap forward in the quality of our employees."

"We're seeing just the first ripples of a wave that is coming in the wishes of employees," Johnson believes. "Good managers must be sensitive to people's needs if they want to attract a competent work force. We're going to have to be more imaginative and less demanding in order to attract the best people."

Employers like Paul Johnson are still few, but the numbers will grow if they realize that it is to their own best interest to take advantage of the talents of mothers (and fathers) who have strong obligations to their own families as well as to their work.

It is up to every mother and father, present and future, to work toward more flexible hours and an enlightened business community that recognizes the strains on the family and the importance of meeting new needs. If more companies get the message, we will be able to maintain a better balance between the demands of work and the claims of people—especially little people.

V

Making Marriage Work

Marriage is better than ever. Marriage is worse than ever.

Once our marriages were held together by external ties. Men and women needed each other for practical reasons, husbands to earn a living, wives to cook and clean and take care of the children. It was comparatively easy to make that kind of marriage work. Roles were clearly defined. We always hoped for romance as well, but if each partner held up the practical end of the bargain, the union could survive without love.

Now we have almost completely reversed the pattern. We marry for love. There are washing machines to do the laundry, take-out foods and TV dinners to replace a cook, and women can earn a living today without having to depend solely on a man for support. We marry now because we want to rather than because we have to, and that makes things a great deal more complicated.

Since we marry for love, we expect it to remain constant over the years. Sex is expected to bring mutual satisfaction, not just children. We hope to remain good friends, with common interests. And today we marry hoping that each partner will be able to continue to grow as a person, to search for personal fulfillment while remaining part of the marriage bond, a condition never before placed on our unions.

When a marriage can meet these new and stringent demands, it can be better than anything couples might have dreamed of in the past. When it does not, we can be more disappointed than ever before because our hopes were so high.

Marriage has never been without problems and never will be, since each partner brings along a set of personal problems and preconceptions which must somehow mesh with those of another complex human being. But recently there has been an added difficulty in making it work: It is easy to get out.

Changes in divorce laws were long overdue and have freed many men and women who were trapped in destructive relationships. But the more marriages that end, the more we hear about the rising rates of divorce, the more temptation there is for couples to leave problems behind rather than struggle to work them out.

In fact, the amazing thing with all that is going against marriage is how many unions do survive. Two out of three may be far fewer lasting marriages than in the past, but it is not such a bad batting average given the current odds. Yet we hear little about these good marriages and much about the bad. It is heartening to meet a husband who declares, "My wife is my best friend," or a wife who will state after twenty-two years of marriage, "I could never conceive of living with anyone else," and there are many of them to be found.

Yet these people will freely acknowledge that their own marriages have gone through rough periods over the years. While every marital relationship varies with the individuals involved, there are some predictable trouble spots that occur in almost every relationship. These are most apt to occur when a shift in living patterns is necessary to accommodate changing roles. If adjustments are not worked out, serious problems will ensue.

The first critical period is an obvious one: the first year of marriage, when two people must learn to live as husband and wife. But the second crisis observed by most marriage counselors is an event that many assume will strengthen the marriage bond: the birth of the first child.

"When the baby came," says new father Carl Olson, "out came all the stereotypes about what mothers and fathers are 'supposed' to do, feelings we were hardly aware we had up to then. In spite of understanding my wife's wanting to work, I still find it hard to accept that my son's mother isn't at home taking care of him. And I feel a lot more awkward than I had expected when I try to help take care of the baby. It has caused our first serious quarrels."

"It was the last straw," asserts Ann Marlowe, an attractive single mother. "We were the most mismatched two people who ever got married in the first place. Here I am—casual, a little messy, pretty free about doing what I want to do when I feel like it. So who did I pick to marry? Ted Marlowe, an absolutely straight, uptight guy. Still we were managing OK until I had a child. For me, that meant responsibility all day long and all night, too. I wasn't ready. I didn't think very hard about whether I was going to like being a mother. And when Ted married me, he surely didn't think about how I fit his notion of a proper mother. We never thought to talk about it ahead of time. It was disaster."

A recent study of new parents done at the University of California confirms these couples' experiences. It calls the birth of the first child possibly the most difficult transition the couple will make in their lifetime, and points out that taking on the role of parent and simultaneously changing from couple to three-part family is tumultuous. Each partner must confront his or her idealized version of what a parent should be, while also juggling new systems in work roles and new intrusions on privacy. Couples need to be warned, concluded the study, that this is a normal and natural adjustment.

Once a working pattern is established, however, many modern marriages are shaken when a wife changes the balance of things by deciding to pursue a new career.

"I guess we're a classic case," says Joan Warren, who ended a fifteen-year marriage after she returned to the working world.

> I had spent two years working before we had kids. Then we shared everything—housework, grocery shopping, cooking. When I became a mother and stayed at home, the role playing started. It seemed logical. If I was around all day, didn't it make sense that I would take care of the house? Eventually, as the children got older, I decided to go back to work. John didn't object. But the reality of the change was simply not what we expected. It went a lot deeper than who did the chores.
>
> For ten years I had devoted the better part of my time and interest to the family. Now I had another commitment that interfered. I was excited with my job and was doing well. That did a lot for my ego, but it had just the opposite effect on John. The more involved I got, the less he liked it. He wanted his old wife back.

The adjustments required by changing aspirations of women are new to our era, but marriage counselors see them as just one more in the necessary transitions every couple must expect to deal with over the years. Reverting to living as a couple after children grow up and leave home, shifting patterns to adapt to retirement, even dealing with the periods of boredom that afflict every long-term relationship—these are all part of the natural course of marriage. Many counselors believe that the inherent difficulties in maintaining a relationship are not so different from what they have always been, and that we could handle the new pressures better with a more realistic idea of what to expect and more of the old commitment to staying together "for better or for worse."

"I'm not sure that I see more stress than before," says marriage counselor Jane MacColl. "There has always been stress in marriage. What I do see is more options for the young and more willingness to end a marriage, even after twenty-five or thirty years, because there is somehow more fantasy about the ability to have an ideal relationship. Marriage is not just a prince and princess living happily ever after. Intimate relationships serve purposes other than romance. We need to affirm the value of sharing, of long-term commitment, of feeling that we are not alone."

Though there is no magic prescription for an ailing marriage, and each union has personal elements that make it different from any other, counselors do see four areas that could be improved in almost every relationship. They might be called the "4 C's" of a strong marriage: communication, conflict, change and commitment. And they are well worth delving into in further detail.

• The Four C's

> I got married when I was twenty-four years old, and I knew absolutely nothing about the realities of living with another person. I certainly got no idea from my parents. They did all their arguing, all their loving, all their decision making in private. In front of the kids, everything was

supposed to be pleasant. That's the way *they* were brought up. I guess they figured if they had learned to live together after marriage, their children would, too.

Well, I can tell you, it hasn't been easy. Not with the problems that come with marriage today. It took a lot of unhappiness before we learned to talk honestly and find ways to make things work better for us. Still, I guess we were lucky. I guess a lot of people never learn.

The speaker is Jim Parker, a husband whose eight-year marriage almost went on the rocks. Jim thought that his wife's return to work had triggered their trouble. But when he and Laura Parker went for counseling, they realized that their problems had begun at the very start of the marriage. Yet they had not communicated to each other their feelings about what was wrong.

"We had both come with a lot of romantic ideas of what it would be like to be married. We never told each other what we expected. Yet when our notions didn't prove true, we blamed each other instead of ourselves. Here's just one example. I had to get in front of a marriage counselor before I said out loud to my wife that I wished she would take the initiative in love making once in a while. I thought once I was married, the pressure would be off—I wouldn't always have to be the one to make the advances. But if I didn't make a move, nothing happened. I was disappointed in Laura and she sensed that something was wrong. But she hadn't the slightest idea what it was."

"I just couldn't believe he had never said anything to me in all these years," Laura chimed in. "I just assumed it was better for the woman to wait to be approached. After all, a woman has the option of saying no, or she can say yes to be agreeable even if she doesn't much feel like making love. But I felt it would be putting Jim on the spot to perform if I started things. How could I know that's what he wanted when he never told me?"

Jim and Laura, like most couples, needed to work past their unspoken expectations to arrive at adjustments that were realistic for their own marriage. But this can only happen if feelings are brought out into the open. And one of the reasons couples fail to communicate is because they hesitate to bring up matters that may turn into arguments.

Conflict is something many of us try to avoid, in and out of marriage. We're taught to control our tempers and hold our tongues from the time we are young. We tell our children, "Don't fight," and operate with a determination not to argue in front of our families.

But it isn't possible to be truly intimate with another person unless you can fight with him. Conflicts are an unavoidable part of honest communication. Husbands and wives who boast that they never argue are actually admitting to a lifeless relationship. Conflicts are inevitable between people who live together and frequently can lead to growth in the relationship.

Not only do we hurt our marriages by agreeing not to disagree, but we perpetuate the problem for our children, giving them no experience in constructive ways to solve differences. It's vital for them to know that people who love each other can be angry, even bitter over a particular issue, without threatening their overall relationship.

Expressing feelings honestly can do a great deal to stop small hurts from growing into large resentments. Unless you say "ouch," someone once said, your partner may never know he has stepped on your toe. The time to yell is immediately, before anger builds. Partners who feel free to express their feelings preserve their individual self-respect, something that is essential to a happy union. And constructive fighting builds trust, for it keeps each partner's emotions out on the table where they can be dealt with. Smoldering resentments are the ones that tend to erupt most destructively.

"When we sense that something is wrong with our marriages, we must take the risk of saying so out loud," counselor Jane MacColl advises.

> It is so vital that each partner try to articulate what is missing for him or her, what expectations are not being met. Our mates might be better able to meet our needs if they only knew what they were.
>
> Men and women are raised with very romantic notions of what love and marriage are going to be like, but our culture tends to be counterproductive. It is as if men and women are raised to speak, understand and respect two different languages. Women fantasize about men who will be sensitive and loving. Our work-oriented society, with such high demands on men for achievement, leaves

men fearful or incapable of showing a soft, emotional side of themselves. Asking men who were raised to get to the top, to forget that they hurt, to function no matter what the circumstances, is a very difficult request.

To solve a marital problem, it's wise to assume that you yourself must take responsibility for what is missing in your life and not place blame on another person. Your expectations, not only of your marriage partner but of your marriage itself, may not be realistic. If you identify your expectations then you can sort out hopes and realities. Hopes can be a basis for changing reality. If I hope for greater intimacy rather than expect it, I can decide how to try to create a more intimate environment. And if I *hope* that life will be exciting rather than *expect* my marriage partner to provide all the excitement in life, I may find the development of some interest or talent of my own to be the real issue.

Ideally, we should examine these feelings and attitudes before the problem becomes severe. Socrates once said, "The unexamined life is not worth living." Re-evaluation is good for every marriage. People are creative about solving their problems once they isolate what they are. Our marriages would do better with periodic "checkups" to understand the changing needs of each mate.

As we've noted, one of the great difficulties in marital relations has been the assumption that people will not change. That might have had some validity when lives were shorter and the pace of life was slower, but today most of us have the opportunity to continue to change and develop throughout our lives. Our marriages must allow room for this growth. Part of the commitment to another person must include a genuine desire to foster growth over the years. If we realize that periodic adjustments in the relationship are essential to accommodate these changes, we may be better prepared to deal with them when they occur. And if the rates of growth are not parallel, we may be better able to wait for a mate to catch up.

Some have questioned whether marriage can work for two changing individuals. There are those who say it is too restrictive an institution to permit individual growth within its bounds. They see "serial marriage" partners as more fitted to the times, a mate to go with each new phase of our lives.

But more people believe that the security of commitment to one person remains our best hope for long-term happiness. Among them are David and Vera Mace, former joint executive directors of the American Association of Marriage Counselors, who say, "The great majority of us are deeply dependent for our satisfactions on the warm, reassuring approval and support of others. We are deeply convinced, from our own experience as well as from observations of other good marriages, that true intimacy in the husband-wife relationship enhances rather than curtails the personal freedom of both partners."[11]

Those who share this view see great potential for enrichment and improvement in traditional marriage. They say we would not need to switch marriage partners if we could learn to periodically revitalize the relationship with the mates we have.

People outgrow the roles in which they have been cast. And they grow up. If marriage is to survive these changes, each person must feel confident enough in the relationship to be able to freely express these changed needs without fear of being abandoned.

Marriage counselor Vidal S. Clay tells of a couple who came to her on the verge of divorce:

> The husband, when he was young, wanted a dependent, traditional wife. Now he has grown stronger and no longer needs this kind of woman to bolster his ego. He wants his wife to grow, too. He is asking her to become more assertive and independent, to make more of a life of her own. She is terrified, immobile, unable to make a move. He is waiting for her, going through the counseling with her. But I can see him getting impatient, and she isn't trying to help herself. It is very sad to see.
>
> He said to her, "If we get divorced and you are forced to go out in the world on your own, you'll become strong and independent. And then you'll be just the sort of woman I need. Can't we do this together? Grow together?" The question is whether she can find the strength to change or whether she will lose her marriage. The potential for saving it is there.

Some psychologists refer to the kind of change that could occur here as "serial monogamy." They point out that marriages pass through cycles of gratifying the needs of both partners and are experienced as fulfilling until one changes and creates an impasse. It is at that point that the danger of divorce may occur. But there is also the possibility that the couple can solve this conflict through communication and good will, struggling together to evolve a new relationship that preserves the old patterns which are still meaningful but makes room for the new.

Since it can be difficult for two people to have enough perspective to see solutions on their own in times of stress, many marriage counselors advocate that couples seek preventive counseling as well as group experiences with other couples designed to deepen their relationships and aid their growth before a crisis occurs. Such group experiences are being offered right now at family service agencies, educational institutions and churches throughout the country, often under the name of "marriage encounters." Even couples who have approached such experiences skeptically report many positive results in improved communication as well as in the reassuring discovery that their problems, which they had thought unique, are common to many marriages.

A number of young people today, perhaps wary of permanent ties because of the rising divorce rates, are postponing marriage and choosing to live together without legal ties. This is another development viewed with alarm by those who fear for the future of the traditional family. Yet a lot of these couples do go on to marry, saying that their decision was based on firmer ground because they had had the opportunity to know each other intimately. Even when the arrangement does not work out, the participants feel they have learned valuable lessons through the experience about the realities of living with another person.

True closeness for most of us continues to require the final commitment that marriage vows bring. Marriage might have been simpler once, but living with another person has never been easy. Many who have experienced divorce have found that it only presents new problems. The important thing for those who want to keep their marriages strong is to remember that there are no problem-free solutions. Concentrating on the important "four C's" of a healthy marriage may help along the way:

Communication

Never assume that your partner knows what you are feeling. Even people who have lived together for years can be amazingly unaware of things that are bothering their mates or of changes in values and needs with passing years. Keep the lines of communication open to allow closeness to continue to grow.

Conflict

Understand that no two people in the world can live together without occasional conflict. Part of successful communication is learning how to disagree constructively rather than harboring resentments that can create serious distance between partners. It is absolutely essential that husband and wife take the risk of bringing their feelings out into the open if they are to find successful ways to deal with the inevitable differences in even the best of marriages.

Change

In a healthy marriage today, each partner must feel free to develop as a person without fear of rejection from husband or wife. Realize that change is a desirable part of life, the spice that keeps us alive and growing. It is not always possible for mates to change together, but it *is* possible for an understanding spouse to be willing to try to adapt to new situations when they represent needs that are important. By keeping in touch with each other's changing needs, we are better able to wait through periods of change to establish a new status quo, rather than rushing to the conclusion that we are no longer suited to our partners.

Commitment

The old-fashioned notion of commitment remains the most important single element in maintaining a good marriage. There are periods in most marriages when it may seem simpler to think of separating than to do the work necessary to remain together. But the rewards of this work are well worth the effort. Reaffirming the value of long-term commitment, of the joys of sharing and compromise and working through problems, is as important as stressing the romance in marriage. It is commitment that makes it possible to work harder through the bad times in order to remain together for the better.

VI

Raising Children Today

Two things stand out about parents raising children today: how much things have changed—and how little.

It has long been part of the American dream to provide a better life for our children than the one we have known, and today's parents continue to work toward this goal. Because we want so much for our families, because we care so much, we fret—just as parents always have—about whether we are doing the best things to help our children along their way. Parents are still debating, as did their parents and grandparents before them, whether children are better off with a strict or a permissive upbringing. There is still a generation gap and we still worry about how best to prepare children for a world that is quite different from the one in which we were raised.

But being a parent today brings some problems that are unique to our times. Because families are often smaller and the generations tend to live further apart, because our neighborhoods tend to be segregated by age group, many of us spend little time with young children until we have our own. We become parents with little conception of what is involved and little training for the task. The kind of advice that was once routinely passed on from mother to daughter is not so readily available to young mothers today. As we've seen, many young women are vocal in expressing feelings of isolation and uncertainty, and a need that never existed before—a need for reassurance about the value of motherhood.

Families are feeling enormous financial pressures. These are brought on by continued inflation, by the "buy, buy" attitude fostered by the advertising that pervades our lives, and by the increasingly accepted notion that a college education is almost a necessity for both boys and girls to succeed in a highly technical and specialized workplace. The need for more income accounts for much of the increase in numbers of working mothers.

Whether mothers work primarily for pay or for personal satisfaction, there is a necessary change in their accustomed roles and less time to spend with their children. Fathers, pressured by their own job demands, also find that time for family is in short supply, even though they are often asked to play a larger role at home.

Time for parental guidance seems doubly important because so many other people influence our youngsters today. Children, too, spend more and more time away from home in school, activities and friendships that may be totally removed from their parents. From their earliest years, they acquire via TV notions about life-styles and values that may be totally different from what they learn at home. We retain responsibility for our children, but we seem to have less authority over them.

Of all the things troubling parents, this outside influence seems paramount. Many express dismay at a society that seems filled with violence, unrest and an unhealthy stress on selfish self-fulfillment. "There used to be certain values you could safely pass on, knowing they were reinforced by school and church and society in general," one thoughtful mother commented. "But now there seems so little discipline or respect in the schools, there is much less religious influence and there's so much emphasis on 'doing your own thing' regardless of other people. How do you teach old-fashioned values at home if children see them ignored everywhere else?"

"There are so many more options, so many new temptations," a father feels. "It's hard to know what to tell children."

A lot of parents feel that they need new kinds of education to guide their children effectively. A recent Gallup poll revealed that three out of four parents approve the idea of adding courses for parents as a regular part of the public school program. They expressed most concern with information about drugs, smoking and alcohol—and indicated willingness to pay additional school taxes if necessary to support such a program.

Sex, traditionally a difficult communication area between generations, is another topic that has become more complicated because of changing standards. "I grew up believing that sex should go with love and marriage," says Ann Archer, the mother of two daughters in their early teens. "I still feel it is not something to be taken lightly, that emotional responsibility should go with an intimate physical relationship. Yet I'm told that young people view things differently today. I know parents who freely allow their college age sons and daughters to bring girl friends and boyfriends home to share their bedrooms. What will I say to my daughters if that time comes? Will they be able to understand my feelings or will they just find my thinking hopelessly outdated?"

Family counselors find that this kind of erosion of parental confidence is common and too often results in an abdication of authority, leaving children without benefit of opinions from anyone except their peers. In many ways, society has become so youth-oriented that unsure parents sometimes seem to be imitating their teenage children in dress and life-style, rather than vice versa. But while we may hesitate to pass on standards and rules we fear are no longer valid, it is just this kind of serious discussion of values and beliefs that children need most today, experts believe.

• Offering Direction

"One of the legitimate functions of a parent is to offer directions and set limits," counsels Mary Corcoran, associate director of a family service agency. "That has not changed. It is so important for parents to let children know what they believe and why. The children need not agree. Nor need the parents feel they must put up a totally confident front, overruling any other point of view. There is no reason not to air your uncertainties about the times. It will free children to be more open with you about their own feelings and doubts."

But while they need the chance to exchange views, children need even more the example of adults who live by their own convictions. Communication can go a long way, but there comes a point at which it must be replaced by action, advises a committee report on parenting issued by the Group for the Advancement of Psychology, an organization of 300 psychiatrists. In answer to Ann Archer and the many parents like her who wonder whether to force their own values on their children, the report urges parents to stand firm, stating: "An example is the college girl who brings her boyfriend home and demands that they be allowed to sleep together in her bedroom. It is within the daughter's values not to be hypocritical, and she is being true to herself in taking this position. It is not within the mother's values to condone this behavior, and she finally has to say (in order to be true to herself), 'You may sleep with your boyfriend if you wish, but not in my house.' Holding the line can be an act of love."[12]

No matter how many others may influence them, youngsters continue to identify most strongly with the most significant persons in their early lives, their parents. They absorb what they observe and are taught at home. There will be a natural period of rebellion and testing as adolescents go through the necessary pulling away to develop into independent adults, but it is high standards and positive expectations at home that ultimately enable young people to transform discipline imposed by parents into the kind of self-discipline that allows them to exercise responsible judgment on their own.

A study of 200 highly successful college students asked what in their backgrounds or life experience had kept these young people on an effective and goal-oriented path. The great majority mentioned family as the most important motivation, adding that their home lives had given them a strong sense of who they were because there were high expectations of all family members. This was true regardless of the family's financial means. Consistency between what parents practiced and preached and firmness in discipline without extremes were named as important elements in producing the inner incentives that lead young people to succeed.[13]

The importance of discipline and limits at home is magnified just because they are so often missing elsewhere today. Children continue to need ground rules. They need to learn to accept responsibility for their own behavior and how to meet rightful obligations. They should be expected to conform to parental standards until they are mature enough to establish standards of their own.

Some elements of responsible parenting never change. Every parent has a right and a duty to know where children are spending their outside time and with whom. For teenagers, curfews, questions about chaperones and an expectation of responsibly moderate behavior are not outdated. Though youngsters may complain outwardly about your concern, on a deeper level it is welcomed. Lack of control can be translated as lack of interest, and every child needs the security of knowing that his parents consider him worthy of concern.

Many authorities believe that stronger parental reactions can help young people cope better with some of the temptations they will face. "If I were to pick one key area of the future, I would look to the family as the main bulwark against drug abuse," stated Dr. Robert L. Dupont, director of the National Institute on Drug Abuse, in a recent speech. "Parents have been neutral on the subject and have essentially backed off.... This must change. Parents must draw the line and be very forceful about limits."[14]

"What parents need most of all," notes Mary Corcoran, "is renewed confidence in their own instincts. They need strengthening in the validity of their personal value system. Just as couples with marital problems feel reassured when they discover their problems and concerns are common to many others, parents who come together to share their uncertainties gain tremendously from the experience, Ms. Corcoran observes. Family service agencies, which have long offered help to families in trouble, are responding to the "confidence crisis" of today's families by providing group sessions for parents who are not having serious difficulties but need the chance to air questions about their everyday family decisions. This new kind of group helps mothers and fathers to clarify their own best directions by talking out options with other parents. This is best done in small groups where everyone feels comfortable to speak up, counselors have found. Such groups are available to families in almost every community today.

• Strength in Numbers

Whether in groups organized for them or by coming together on their own, many parents have found that joint endeavors also help to solve some of the more practical problems that they cannot handle alone. From gathering to discuss infant care to fighting violence in the schools, parents are taking constructive kinds of action that may offer new ideas and even a bit of inspiration.

One new kind of group is springing up to help young mothers, providing places where they can share their child-rearing concerns while their children learn to socialize with one another.

The Parents Workshop in New York City is such a place. With a trained leader to guide them, parents here clarify their own values and explore different parenting styles.

"It was so good to find out that there are many different ways of going about things, that no one way is right or wrong, that children differ—and most of all, that most of us feel the same way and share the same insecurities," one participant comments. "Here, I feel free to ask 'dumb' questions that I'm embarrassed to call my pediatrician about. These are all mothers just like me. They understand."

A similar program operates at the Infant-Toddler-Parent Center in Pacific Oak, California. Three young mothers in Stamford, Connecticut, feeling the same kind of need for reassurance, took a more long-range approach to their parenting concerns. They wrote up a proposal for funding of the Stamford Family Life Workshops covering many phases of the growing-up years and applied successfully to a local philanthropic foundation for a small grant to fund the project.

"I became interested in the idea because of my past experience with a La Leche group as preparation for breast-feeding my child," says Rosalea Fisher, one of the founders of the Workshops.

> I realized that those meetings had served two purposes. They were dealing with feeding, but they were also preparing us for the experience of being a parent and helping us to understand what parenting is all about.
>
> There was no equivalent after the baby was born. We began with some of the same mothers who had gone to La Leche together, meeting twice monthly with our children to compare notes on the

"trivial" things like diapering, feeding, naps and so forth that were suddenly such an important part of our lives. We also discussed such issues as discipline, sibling rivalry, nutrition and health. Our aim was to provide a forum where we could exchange viewpoints and techniques with a trained leader to help us.

Realizing that each new stage of child development is a new experience for a mother, the group over a period of years has had sessions on toddlers, nursery-school-age children, how to understand and react to children's behavior, adolescents, working mothers and single parents. The Workshops, open to all, are held in nursery schools, school buildings, churches, community centers and at the local library. "Our grant pays for the workshop leaders, publicity and postage," Ms. Fisher says. "A project like ours could run for perhaps a thousand dollars a year. But the need it serves is invaluable. To give you an idea of why this is so important, one participant at a meeting for working mothers just sat and never said a word. She was only contemplating a return to work and needed help clarifying whether she was ready. Afterwards she told us that hearing the actual experiences of other women helped her to make up her mind."

The Family Life Workshops help fulfill another necessary function, Ms. Fisher believes. "We hear so much about working, so little about mothering as a profession. Our group tries to help women who want to be full-time mothers to feel that it is still a worthwhile course to pursue."

Mothers with common concerns are finding other solutions to the problems they face. Those who want to work but worry about the quality of available day care sometimes band together to start their own facilities. In *The New Extended Family*, authors Ellen Galinsky and William H. Hooks describe a number of centers that have been organized and run by parents. One of these is the Bank Street College Center, which Ms. Galinsky herself helped to start.

As she describes her day with her young daughter, "I was just seeing her out of her pajamas in the morning and again into her pajamas at the end of a long day."[15]

She wondered if parents who worked near the Bank Street College building could somehow organize a program for their infants and toddlers closer to work, where they might be able to drop by on a break or join their children for lunch. The college was lukewarm to the idea at first, but with persistence the parents were finally given a basement room for their use, rent-free.

The Center has been able to operate solely on tuition fees, thanks to supplementary fund-raising efforts by the sponsoring parents. They use secondhand furniture, make their own repairs and seek donations of used toys. The one area in which they will not compromise is in the quality of the staff caring for their children. Their active involvement in their children's daily care makes them feel a lot easier about leaving the youngsters each day.

Another group of parents has partially solved the problem of what to do with school-age children whose parents are still at work after three o'clock. "We knew that there were more and more of us working and sharing this problem, yet the school closed down and sent these kids home," said Barbara Riley, one of the plan's originators. "Many of our kids were too old to need sitters but too young for no supervision at all. So we formed a committee. First we petitioned the Board of Education, but they told us there was an insurance problem. Then we tried a church near the school. They were more sympathetic. We hired a teacher to set up games and projects for the kids and inaugurated an after-school program within walking distance of the school."

• Parent Participation

Even if they cannot actually run the program, parents can be more vitally involved in what happens to their children if they will work more closely with school personnel to see that children have a positive experience, believes Jeanne Ellis, director of a day care center:

> Day care properly should be a supplement to parenting. Rather than a minus, it can add interaction and stimulation beyond what any mother can offer at home. But it is up to the parent to see that they share in this part of the child's life. As early

childhood educators, we have the opportunity to be very influential in establishing good healthy patterns for children. But we are effective only when parents work with us for these goals.

We expect parents to come to meetings, to express themselves, to know the child's teachers and to help us know their child better. Children need to know that what they do all day is important to their parents. Our purpose is not to replace the family but to support it. Whether we are successful depends in large part on the parents themselves.

If parents want more good facilities for child care, they can't sit back and wait for others to do that for them, either. They must get to their own community planners and make their needs known.

Parent participation remains the key to success in later schooling as well, believes Terry H. Bell, former U.S. Commissioner of Education. Those who feel helpless in influencing schools are wrong, Bell said in a recent interview, for the best schools are located in neighborhoods where parents are actively involved and where schools reach out to encourage parental participation.[16]

Parents can make a difference on many levels. In one New England elementary school, mothers determined to stretch a limited school budget to turn the school library into an up-to-date multimedia center. They raised money, solicited donations of equipment and provided the volunteer manpower to put the center into operation. It proved so popular with students that it was adapted eventually as a model for the entire school system.

In Miami, Florida, parents intervened in another area, becoming paid counselors in an experiment to fight delinquency in five local high schools. "I am convinced," says Sam Moncur, director of the parent program, "that a lot of the disruptive behavior in the schools goes on because the kids think their parents won't know about it."[17] Now, with parents riding buses, checking on students who are habitually late, counseling students and visiting their homes, the youngsters seem less likely to cause trouble. "From 1975 through 1977, our school had the highest number of violent acts in the county,"[18] reports Matthew Lawrence, assistant principal at Miami Central Senior High School. "This year, the figures have been reduced drastically."

Busy parents today may have little time to volunteer at school and only a handful can work where their children are, but every parent can find time to know his children's teachers, to be aware of and show interest in what each child is doing in school. Parental concern remains the crucial difference in providing incentive for learning. Studies of high school dropouts coming from the same kinds of home environments show how much home life affected whether a child stayed in school. Four out of five dropouts came from homes where there was little communication or parental interest in school affairs and where the family seldom participated in any kind of activities together.

• Finding Time for Family

Most parents recognize the importance of spending time together as a family, but even the best intentioned can find it difficult because of the large number of outside demands on their time. Families seem fully aware of the problem, particularly those with working mothers. When asked how they are changing things to find more time for family, working mothers most typically replied that they were lowering their housekeeping standards, eating out more often or bringing more prepared foods in. More important, they were learning to make the most of short periods of time. Says one mother, "While I'm mending or doing the wash, sewing or paying bills, I ask one or more of the kids to help. I find that this kind of natural, companionable time together gives them the chance to open up to me. I used to shut myself off from them when I was busy with chores."

"Fifteen minutes with each child before bedtime pays huge dividends," a father declares. "It's a relaxed kind of time together and seems a perfect time for confiding."

Another father says that taking his children to school each day has given him an extra few minutes to get to know them better.

Some busy families have found another solution, a formal "family hour" for getting together regularly.

"We were going in so many different directions, I began to realize that we were rarely all home together at the same time, relates Jane Frank, a midwestern mother of four.

> Cal, my husband, travels a lot. When he is home, he's very active with the scouting program here. I have a part-time job and many volunteer commitments. First thing you know, we were giving more time to other people's kids than to our own.
>
> As for the kids, their schedules are unbelievable, between practices, meetings, games and dates. When we were together, the kids were likely to eat and run, either to get somewhere or even just to get to the TV set. We just decided something had to be done. So we declared Thursday as family night. It sounds artificial, I know. After dinner each person would go over what had gone on in their lives that week so we could all share. At the start it was strained, but after a time it really began to work. The kids would ask questions about our work, we'd go into what they had covered in class or their outside activities. Sometimes that would lead to discussions of politics, or philosophies or teaching methods or morals—you just can't believe that something like this could have opened up so much more communication. We've been able to talk out some family squabbles as well. And we seem to do a lot more talking every day of the week now because we've grown in closer touch with each other. If it takes making an appointment to see your family these days, it's well worth the effort.

Many other families have adopted a similar plan, some coming together for an informal Sunday-night dinner, others finding Saturday or Sunday breakfast an ideal time for relaxed communication.

• Turning Off the TV

A few pioneer families have found big blocks of new time for family activities by turning off the television set. TV seems to occupy inordinate numbers of hours for people of all ages, and many families agreed that it has gotten out of hand. "It's true," one mother admitted sheepishly. "Almost any night you can come in and find all of us sitting in the room, side by side, not speaking a word to each other, just watching some silly show on TV as though it were the most important thing any of us had to do."

Some educators have become so concerned about the effects of excessive television watching on children that they have actually requested that parents cut off their youngsters' time with the tube. In September 1977, the Board of Education in Niagara Falls, New York, unanimously adopted a resolution urging families "to choose television programs more carefully and to limit the viewing so that pupils will make the best possible use of their time and talents."[19] Kimberton Farms School in Pennsylvania also recently asked parents to ban all TV for children in nursery school, kindergarten and first grade, and to keep children in grades 2 through 12 away from the set Sunday through Thursday nights.

But while recognizing the problem, most parents are slow to act on it. They confess that they depend on the set as a baby-sitter—and are often addicted themselves.

Yet those brave souls who have restricted television in their homes, while admitting that it was a difficult adjustment in many ways, firmly proclaim that the ultimate benefits are worth the withdrawal pangs.

"We read in our house again," says Donald Carter, the father of three sons, ages 9, 11 and 14. "We sit longer at the dinner table. We talk more. The kids have taught us how to play backgammon and we have family tournaments that are really fun for all of us. Before, we were all glued to the TV set for most of our spare hours. You just don't realize how it restricts your life until you force yourself to stop. At first we cut out all TV, but now we do watch the worthwhile specials and the big sports events. The thing is, we've broken the habit of automatically sitting down to watch every night. It has given us many more hours for doing things together."

Schools can caution or recommend, but the TV controls remain firmly in the hands of the family. Using them more sparingly is something every parent concerned with finding time for family would do well to consider.

• Learning to Help

Schools have led the way for parents in still another area, showing how children can be taught to be part of a solution to finding more free time for family. At the Norwood Avenue Elementary School in Cranston, Rhode Island, principal Marie Lawrence began to notice that more children were coming to class with buttons missing and hems undone because working mothers had not had the time to tend to the mending. It occurred to Mrs. Lawrence that if mothers could not find time for all the chores that needed doing, the children could learn to do more for themselves. She and her staff developed Project HELP, a series of workshops and demonstrations that taught children how to use a stove, washer, vacuum cleaner, kitchen utensils, carpentry tools, scissors, needle and thread. They were also given information on nutrition and taken on shopping field trips to supermarkets.

One mother's surprised reaction: "I thought my kids were too young to do anything at home. I used to rush through all the housework weekends and be exhausted. Now one child does the wash for me during the week, another makes school lunches. They both help with dinner. If we need things from the store, I'm confident that either can find what we need in the supermarket and know how much they should get for their money. That saves me from shopping on my way home in the rush hour."

The program proved so successful it has been expanded and is now sponsored by the Rhode Island State Department of Education. Teachers noted that the children's self-confidence bloomed as they learned more about taking care of themselves.

Many mothers have learned in their own homes that youngsters who are given more responsibility at home feel better about themselves as individuals. Once we automatically expected children to be productive family members, but today it is the exception to expect them to share the workload. Yet in families that have restored their youngsters to an active role in taking care of the household, the dividends reported are many, not the least of which is a closer family relationship overall. One mother, Evelyn Sims, describes it as "being partners."

"We took this seriously," she relates, "sat down together at a formal family meeting and discussed how we could rearrange things to share the work more evenly. The children had to be taught a lot of things, like cooking and how to work appliances properly, and there were mistakes at first. But now they are proud of their accomplishments. They have helped free me to do more pleasant things with them—and when we do the work together, even that turns into happy times together very often. The spirit of cooperation that grew up has spilled over into other areas of our relationships. Sharing responsibilities, making decisions as a family group, trusting the children and expecting them to understand our needs—all of these things have led to better and better communications between us."

FAMILY COMMUNICATION

In every area of our family lives, honest communication is a vital element. Because we do tend to spend less time together, it becomes even more important that we improve the quality of time we do share by examining some of the roadblocks that commonly develop to prevent the open expression of feelings.

According to family counselors, one of the primary problems is something we have already recognized as a stumbling block in marital relationship: unrealistic expectations.

We become parents with a lot of preconceived ideas about how children ought to behave, but these ideas may have little in common with the way real children do behave. Nor will our children necessarily flatter us by turning out to be just like us or help us compensate for our shortcomings by succeeding where we failed. If our hopes are for a sweet compliant child, a star athlete, a scholar or a "most likely to succeed," and the reality is just the opposite, we often let our children know our disappointment in a dozen subtle ways. They sense our dissatisfaction, but not understanding the reasons, they withdraw. Only if we examine our feelings and recognize the problem we may be creating can we adjust our behavior to reality and begin accepting our children the way they really are.

Children, too, have their share of expectations about the way parents ought to behave. They would like to know that they can be sure of a sympathetic hearing rather than anger if they get into trouble, would like less pressure about grades, wish parents would be more understanding about their peer pressures.

Parents may not always live up to these ideals, but we might come closer if we were aware of our children's wishes. They are seldom articulated, however, because to do so might risk anger or rejection from parents. "There's no use talking to Mom or Dad," they say. "They'll just get mad."

Its up to the parent to create the kind of open climate that makes it possible for everyone to feel freer to express feelings. Often all it takes is simply to tell our children honestly what we hope to do. Then we must live up to our promises and listen without passing hasty judgments. If we will accept our children and try to see things more from their point of view, in time we may merit this same kind of trusting reception from them.

And while we can't approve all of our children's actions, we can avoid condemning feelings. If we respond to confidences with comments such as "You shouldn't feel that way," or to expressions of emotions with statements such as "Big boys and girls don't cry," we are only hindering further sharing. Particularly where our sons are concerned, we have a real opportunity to help break the pattern that has kept men afraid to admit to their emotions. By providing a home where all kinds of feelings and interests are respected, we can help boys to grow into warm and loving men who are not afraid to express what they feel.

For boys and girls alike, it is important that all interests, whether in arts, or science, carpentry or sports, be encouraged and recognized so that children will be able to develop in their own most fulfilling directions, free of old rigid stereotypes about what is masculine and feminine.

Actions always speak louder than lectures, so if we want to teach our children to express themselves, we must learn to be more expressive ourselves. We must allow our children to see us when we are feeling angry, frightened or sad so that they understand better how to deal with these emotions. A child's education for marriage should begin in the home, where we allow him to see the compromises, the routine and the conflict that are unavoidable facts of life. Wearing a pleasant neutral mask in front of our children is a common parental path, but it discourages true intimacy. Our children must feel they really know us before they can trust us.

Part of letting youngsters know us better is to share with them some of the serious concerns of the family. "Too many parents just won't talk openly to their children," observes Margaret Murta, director of a family service agency. "Parents don't consider the children old enough to be included in important family discussions. Very often we see parents who are having difficulties which they believe they are keeping from their children. We always ask that the children be brought in on matters that will affect them. In truth, there are no 'family secrets.' I can't tell you

103

how often I've seen parents amazed to learn that six-year-old Johnny has sensed problems they thought they had carefully kept from him."

One technique that can help us in getting in touch with each other is called "feedback." This means actively asking for reactions to our behavior. So often we antagonize each other without even knowing it, and if we can begin to understand better how others feel about the way we behave, we may be able to do a great deal to improve family relations.

Many families have found that this kind of feedback occurs most easily at a regularly scheduled family meeting where everyone is encouraged to speak what is on his or her mind. These meetings can often resolve small disputes before they mushroom into large problems. Meetings can determine equitable rules about borrowing possessions, for example, or penalties mutually agreed upon in advance for chores left undone. They are an ideal opportunity to openly discuss problems and let everyone participate in finding solutions. As we've seen, in some families they become the source of a new system of cooperation in sharing responsibilities more fairly.

Calling meetings may begin as an artificial device, but families who have tried it report that it can develop into an invaluable tool for fostering openness, improved communication and a feeling of family unity.

As with so many matters today, families who are aware of the need for better communication in their homes but unsure how to bring it about are sometimes joining together to seek solutions. One unique attempt at a group setting where whole families can learn to relate more realistically is called the "family cluster," an experiment being tried right now with minor variations by many kinds of organizations across the country.

"The purpose of the 'family cluster' is to help families learn how to communicate better by respecting their children more," says Mark Edison, a leader of a group that meets regularly in a small New England town. "We try to set an example of how families can be run in a way that the participants can apply at home.

> In a typical cluster we have twenty to twenty-five people of all ages from toddlers to grandparents. We meet weekly on Sunday after church. Each family brings a picnic lunch. We do things that everyone can take part in—play games, sing songs, make simple things. The idea is to learn to relax, build a feeling of affection and trust in the group that will allow us eventually to open up and talk about things comfortably together.

> It is not a class. No one is ever corrected or disparaged. No one is ever pressured to talk. But everyone is welcome to participate. We pick simple topics like how each family celebrates a holiday or what kinds of things we like to do. The children are always encouraged to speak up, as well as the adults. It is something they rarely get a chance to do in adult company. Their parents begin to see them in a little different light, to see that even the youngest are individuals with their own points of view.

> You almost have to be there week after week

105

to see how a feeling of affection grows up in the group. It is a nonthreatening atmosphere where everyone feels accepted. After a time together, we are able to talk about things that are more meaningful, problems with adolescents perhaps, or other more personal family matters. The leader is only a gentle force to keep things moving. We always encourage the children to have their say, and the better we get to know each other, the more everyone opens up.

Being a parent is one of the hardest jobs there is. There's no training for it. We're just supposed to know how to operate. And society expects us to be not just good but perfect. We want our children to act in a way that reflects credit back on us in public, to show the world what a good job we are doing. We sometimes forget that these children are individuals, too, and need the chance to express their own needs at home. Children must be listened to as well as talked at. The "family cluster" gives you a new perception of your children. Families go back home with new ideas about how to communicate with their children, as well as warm bonds to other families that are hard to come by in our transient world.

The methods of the "family cluster" are much the same that any individual family would use to foster better communication: openness, acceptance, good will, mutual respect and the assurance of a hearing without judgment.

• In Summary

Some of the dilemmas families face have changed, but the basic elements of good parenting have not.

Children still need the security of parents who stand for something. It is from parental discipline, direction and example that a child develops the kind of strong personal value system that will enable him or her to function as a responsible adult. Parental concern and interest remain the most significant factors in ensuring a child's success in school. And the more we respect our children, accept them and talk openly to them, the more likely they are to respond.

In review, here are some of the ways that counselors and other parents believe that today's parents can become more effective:

Give Your Child High Ideals

Youngsters often develop according to what they feel their parents expect of them. Regardless of what may be happening in the outside world, if your expectations for your children are high, your good opinion of them will encourage them to set high standards for themselves.

Set a Good Example

It does no good to preach values if you do not live according to the principles you espouse. Don't give your children conflicting messages.

Provide Reasonable Limits

Concern for your child's welfare is never old-fashioned. Every child needs direction and rules from his parents. Don't hesitate to impose the discipline you feel is appropriate, regardless of what you may be told other parents are doing.

Become Involved in Your Child's Schooling

Make a point of knowing your children's teachers so that you can help them to know the children better. Show your interest by keeping current on your child's school work and praising his accomplishments. Rather than complaining if you don't like the way the schools are run, find out whether your time and talents might contribute to making things better.

Improve Family Communication Techniques

Recognize the unrealistic expectations that may be undermining your relationships, work to establish an open accepting climate and try to set up a pattern of "feedback" to give a more accurate reflection of feelings between family members.

Find a Support Group

Once parental support and guidance came more naturally from family and neighborhood ties. Today many families find substitute concern from other parents who share their dilemmas. Whether the need is for instruction, practical help or simply the chance to air uncertainties and clarify values, individual families frequently find they can find solutions best by working together.

Find Time for Family

Spending time together is essential if you hope to create close and meaningful family relationships.

In large and small ways, analyze your own family patterns for possible changes that may result in more time for family. In this busy era, it seems beneficial to designate specific times for regular family discussions. There is no way to communicate if you aren't together!

VII

Special Families

SINGLE PARENTS

When we talk about families, it was once understood that we were talking about mothers and fathers raising their children together. For millions of families today, however, someone is missing from that picture.

With a million divorces occurring every year, the number of children who live with only one parent has increased dramatically. Enough of these divorces involve youngsters to propel a million children into new kinds of living arrangements. Right now it is estimated that as many as one out of every six children lives in a home with only one parent or relative present.

In acknowledgment of the growing numbers, we've added a new term to our vocabularies. No longer do we refer to "broken homes." Instead we talk about "single-parent families," a kind of recognition that millions of mothers and fathers bringing up their children alone are still running a family after all—and often running them very well.

But there is no denying that being a single parent brings many extra burdens. Providing the kind of security, discipline and guidance children need to thrive, creating a climate of trust and open communication and, most of all, finding time for family concerns can be much more difficult with no second parent present to lend either practical assistance or moral support.

If traditional families are suffering from an erosion of confidence, single parents feel this problem many times over, magnified by their sense of isolation.

We hear so much about this new kind of lifestyle that it becomes easy to overestimate its prevalence. In spite of the growth in numbers, single-parent families comprise only 15 percent of the total number of family units in America. And old steroptypes die hard. So the men and women who find themselves living the part of single parent in a society that is still overwhelmingly couple-oriented feel a frightening sense of loneliness at the start—and often a pervading sense of guilt.

The guilt is present even when the family's new status was caused by death. When it is a case of divorce, which seems to imply failure on the part of the parents, the guilt can be so heavy as to be damaging to both parent and child.

"I've never felt so completely alone," says suburban single mother Sandra King.

When I got a divorce, I knew of other families who had split, but I had no idea what had become of them. All of my friends were still married, and for all that they were sorry and wanted to help, they simply had no idea of what I was going through.

I was overcome with remorse for my children. The first night my husband was gone, I went upstairs to tuck the children into bed and found myself sobbing. Here were these innocent children and look what I had done to them—left them without a father because I had made such a mess of things. Realistically, that was absurd. My husband had gone off to marry another woman. Still, I felt like a failure to my children. For the longest time I bent over backwards trying to make it up to them somehow. They could have become spoiled brats if I hadn't gotten some perspective and realized what I was doing.

Many newly single parents do fall into the trap of trying to overcompensate. They may hesitate to enforce discipline, deny themselves a social life to devote extra time to the children, give too many presents and give in to too many demands. It's a common pattern for the parent at home to try to preserve for the youngsters a life exactly as it was when both parents were present, even though new circumstances often suggest major changes.

Trying to maintain the old status quo never works for long because it puts the remaining parent in the position of trying to be two people, filling a void that cannot be filled. Children inevitably must come to terms with the loss of a parent and realistic new patterns must be established. Much to the surprise and relief of troubled parents, the new honesty and sharing brought on by the need to adjust to changes may be a catalyst for improved family relations.

"After a shaky start, our daily family life has really changed for the better," says Denise Morris, a single mother of three. "First of all, this was probably the first time in my life I had leveled with the children about my problems. I had to get a job. I was petrified. The kids became my biggest boosters and really helped see me through it. We began helping each other in lots of ways we hadn't before, became more "interdependent," you might say. We aren't afraid to speak up now when we need help. Needing one another has brought us closer."

The new openness that results from a family crisis can have another unexpected benefit. Ironically, some children find that they come to know their parents better after they no longer live under the same roof.

"My daughter tells me that the divorce has improved her relations with us," says Angela Todd, mother of a thirteen-year-old. "She never thought of us as two separate people when we were living together. Now she must relate to us as individuals, sees us more clearly and says she feels closer to each of us because she knows us better. I'm sorry it took a divorce to bring this about, but it does make me feel a lot better about things. It also gives me some very welcome time to myself when I know my daughter is well taken care of and happy with her father."

Divorce separates mothers and fathers, but it need not separate them from their children. Parents who allow their children to continue to love and receive love from both parents are doing a great deal to diminish the traumas of separation. It is not the divorce itself that is destructive. In fact, many professionals like child psychologist Louise Despert believe that a clean break can be far less damaging than what she terms "emotional divorce," the state that exists in so many homes where parents remain together though they have ceased to care for each other.

"The most serious danger," she believes, "lies in depriving them of the emotional support they must have to grow on. They can be deprived of all material luxuries, even of many physical comforts and yet thrive and grow to wholesome maturity if their emotional needs are satisfied.... A child can absorb and survive almost any painful experience if he is sure of his family's love."[20]

Nothing is more important to children than meaningful relationships with the parent who has left, usually meaning the father. It falls to this parent to reassure them of his love and concern. This is best accomplished by trying to make the children feel a welcome part of the new life he has established, including them in his normal activities rather than planning special outings or entertainment when he sees them. Youngsters don't need this kind of guilt-ridden and artificial entertaining. They need the same kind of healthy personal

115

concern and open communication as they did when their parents lived together. Spending time in the father's home doing routine things such as making dinner together builds far more rapport than expensive outings.

When lingering bitterness between parents or death or desertion makes it impossible for children to have the participation of both parents in their lives, many single parents are able to substitute meaningful role models and relationships through the growing network of single parent organizations. The pioneer group of this kind, Parents Without Partners, has more than 900 chapters across the country. The members meet to discuss common problems in raising children alone, to share misgivings or questions about their new lifestyle as well as to have good times together, with and without their children.

As the number of single parents grows, the number of services to help them also multiplies. Community centers, family counseling services and churches of all denominations have initiated many helpful supports. In Birmingham, Alabama, for example, there are organizations for single parents at the Baptist Church as well as the Jewish Community Center, both open to all denominations. The St. Peter's Catholic Church is planning a series of retreats for its divorced members.

In Flushing, New York, the Single Parent Family Center at the Greater Flushing YM-YWHA provides clothing swaps, food co-ops, baby sitting pools, group vacation trips and potluck suppers, the latter proving a special boon to divorced parents whose dinner hours may be painfully void of adult company.

The Lenox Hill Neighborhood Association in Manhattan has established a "hot line" where single mothers can find a sympathetic ear when things go wrong. Those who answer are other single mothers who know how it feels when husbands are gone, parents live far away and married friends no longer understand.

Single parents of both sexes often join together for happier reasons. Ski houses are traditionally rented by groups of single people. In Great Barrington, Massachusetts, and Jamaica, Vermont, there are houses shared by single men and women—plus their children of all ages. The groups share expenses, divide cooking duties, keep an eye on one another's children and form many warm and lasting friendships. Another group has shared a summer vacation house on Long Island Sound for eight years, with a waiting list on tap to fill in for those who defect by rejoining the marrieds.

When married couples become aware of the painful isolation of the single-parent families in their midst, a new kind of group may develop. Called an "intentional family," it is an attempt to bring together people of all ages and marital status in an ongoing relationship that provides some of the warmth and support that once came from large extended families. It gives single parents the chance to offer their children new role models without the complications of a romantic relationship.

"My little girl was absolutely dying for male attention. I could see it whenever a date came to the house," says Jeannette Logan, mother of a six-year-old daughter.

My own father adores her but he lives four hundred miles away. I have no other family nearby. What has been wonderful for her and me is the 'intentional family' we joined. It is sponsored by the local Unitarian Church, but is open to anyone.

In my group there are two married couples with families, five single parents and three single people. The ages range from twenty-five to sixty and there are about fifteen children from four to nineteen. We get together regularly for activities like picnics, ball games, skating or sometimes just sharing dinner.

It was stilted until we were together enough to begin to know each other, but after a while you could feel the atmosphere begin to change. All of us agreed that our lives were compartmentalized, that married people see only other married people, singles see only other singles, and we stick with our own age groups. Here was a chance to experience what you'd find in a big old-fashioned family. And in many ways we came to feel like family—some people's personalities clashed, some resented the demands on their time the group entailed. But most of us have been together for two and a half years now and we get so much from it. It's wonderful for Christie—and for me, too. I feel these are men as well as women I can count as true friends, whom I can come to for advice or help if I need it.

When I was married and busy with my own world, I don't think I would have found the time or impetus to get involved in something like an intentional family. Being a single parent has made me so much more aware of the importance of other people in your life. Even if I remarry, I'll never be as shut away inside my own four walls again.

Single parents advising those who are just adjusting to this state recognize the value of reaching out to others. It is the first of three important guidelines they offer:

Don't Hesitate to Ask for and Accept Help When You Need It

Professional counseling has helped families to understand their feelings during this time of stress. Support groups of all kinds are a source of strength, including those that provide social outlets for lonely parents. Both parents and professionals agree that the key to whether children come through the experience without emotional damage is how well the parent can rebuild his or her life. Parents who take care of themselves are best able to take care of their children.

Recognize Self-Defeating Guilt and Fight It

It serves no constructive purpose to try to "make up" to children for the traumas they suffer from death or divorce. The children must make their own adjustments. The most helpful thing a parent can do is to allow them to express openly their natural feelings of anger, fear or disappointment— and their own feelings of guilt for possibly contributing to the break. An open climate of communication is the best gift you can give your child at this time.

For Divorced Parents: Declare a Truce With Your Ex-Mate

If children can continue to enjoy and relate lovingly to two parents, the pains of divorce are greatly minimized. Finding the maturity to work together for their children's best interests also does a great deal to help parents do away with exaggerated guilt feelings.

For most single parents, a period of readjustment before remarriage is advisable. It takes time after a life crisis to regain confidence and find the self-perspective to avoid repeating past mistakes. Rushing into a marriage solely to provide a new father or mother for children may present more problems than it solves. It is better for all if the single parent learns to find strength from within before forming a new serious relationship.

With all its problems, single parenting is an experience that can bring new independence, strength and maturity. It teaches many the importance of sharing their concerns—with their children and with each other. Happily, most single parents find that children are resilient, with a built-in drive toward emotional health that an honest and genuinely loving parent can foster regardless of life's crises.

As single parents grow more confident about themselves and their children, most of them do begin to feel ready to try again to make marriage work. Four out of five divorced people do remarry, as do many who are widowed. And when children are involved, we get still another kind of "intentional family," the stepfamily.

STEPPARENTS

What word best describes the many merged families in our midst?

"Complicated," grins Jim Turner, second husband to Molly, stepfather to her two children and weekend father to his own sons. "If you think marriages are tough adjustments the first time around, just try it with a new wife plus two kids."

Second marriages involving children bring many predictable challenges. On top of the concerns stepparents share with all parents, there is the need to mesh living patterns of well-formed personalities. The Turners are typical of many families when they discuss the day-to-day dilemmas that come with forging a new family unit. Finding comfortable new roles and patterns, personality conflicts, resentments and jealousies are among them.

"I think I have a basically good relationship

with Molly's children, but they have their own father and I can't forget it. I don't feel as free with them as with my own kids. It seems better if their mother is the disciplinarian, but that's not the way it was in either of our first marriages. So we have to shift and learn to live with what seems most workable in a new situation. We go from day to day."

Jim has found that some jealousy is inevitable. "The children had had their mother to themselves for three whole years. They were probably more attached than is normal in a mother-child relationship. I could understand that. And I don't deny there were times when the feeling was reversed—when I resented the kids because I wanted Molly to myself. What we've learned from this is something that is vital if a marriage, second or first, is going to work well—that you must be able to talk freely about what you are feeling. Being honest is what is helping us to survive. We were almost forced into it because of our circumstances, but it is so much healthier than my first marriage in that respect. I have no doubt this family and marriage are ultimately going to be fine."

Molly comments on another facet of the jealousies that can arise. "I can see that Jim has a special feeling for his own children. But I understand that because I do, too, and I would be lying if I said otherwise. When there is a divorce, there is added reason for this. You feel guilty and want to be sure the kids aren't shortchanged for your attentions. The two sets of children sometimes resent each other, but they gain something from this situation, too. They learn to relate to different kinds of people. Jim's kids, for example, have a mother who is a career woman. They love her a lot and find her a stimulating person. Me, I'm a homebody, very different from their mother. But I feel they are learning to care for me, too, not as a mother but as a warm, concerned friend. They like the fact that our house is warm and relaxed and there's lots of home-cooked food around. They see two successful life-styles and can choose which one they want for themselves."

But learning to live with different kinds of people requires effort from children. Those who have grown up with an undemonstrative parent may find it hard to adjust to one who is more emotional. Messy children have problems with neat stepparents, noisy children with quiet ones. Extending families through remarriages requires everyone to become more flexible. There are some conflicts that never will be resolved and simply must be lived with.

"It takes a sense of perspective—and a sense of humor," stepmother Connie Egan notes wryly.

When my husband and I married, we each brought two sons with us. I was divorced, he was widowed. Our boys had known each other and went to the same school, which helped. Still, we have rough times.

Mitchell, my oldest son, used to put himself physically between us whenever he saw Rich hug me. Rich's sons resented the time he gave to my boys. And they had a hard time accepting a replacement for their mother, though I thought I was making progress.

> As a stepmother you have to come to the realization that things may never be totally the way you would like them to be. One night not long ago, my youngest stepson had a bad dream and woke up crying. I went in to comfort him. We had a good long talk that night about a lot of things, and as I sat in a chair hugging him, I felt we had really broken down a barrier in our relationship. When he felt better, we went down and had milk and cookies and laughed a lot together. Then, as I was saying good night, he turned to me and said, "I still like my own mother better than you."
>
> Do you cry or do you laugh? Fortunately, I did understand and most fortunately, I'm able to laugh—at least most of the time.

If life with stepchildren is difficult, parents whose own relationship is sound often find that working on the problems together builds a close bond. So long as the children are not suffering from severe emotional problems, stepfamilies are usually successful over the long haul in creating new bonds and becoming a real family unit. One of the reasons is that stepparents do usually understand that trauma is natural in the situation, so they don't feel personally inadequate when it arises.

Many do consult family advisers for direction when children are causing serious dissension between husband and wife. But while there are exceptions, most stepfamilies do surprisingly well. Dr. Lucille Duberman, a Rutgers University sociologist, studied remarriage among one hundred Ohio families and found that 82 percent of them had achieved a good or excellent relationship, a ratio that would do credit to any group of families.[21]

Perhaps men and women who remarry, having grown and learned from their past mistakes, have more realistic expectations.

"You know the ups and downs of family life," one wife said. "You've gained the experience to understand that misunderstandings pass when there is basic good will. And when things go wrong, you know not to hold back feelings but to talk it out."

Stepparents share the same uncertainties about guiding their children, the same complaints about lack of enough time, particularly because so many mothers must work to help with the financial strains of merging families.

But a lot of these families have learned something that is valuable advice for all families. Circumstances are so different in each stepfamily that few will offer blanket rules to others. The one message they give unanimously, however, is the reminder that some of life's problems cannot be resolved and must be tolerated, that we must always put up with complications and compromises in our lives and that we deal best with our difficulties when we talk about them.

Stepparents who have known the bad and then found good relationships seem the loudest advocates of all for the enduring worth of marriage and family life in spite of the problems. What remains to be solved is how to strengthen our families for the future so that we can reap the rewards of family without having to go through a second time around.

VIII

The Importance of Caring Relationships

There is a house for sale on Suburban Lane.

The occupants, Jerry and Linda Graham and their family, fit almost all of our favorite stereotypes of the "typical American family": a working father and a stay-at-home mother, a son and a daughter, a cat and a dog, a split-level house, a station wagon for Mom and a station car for Dad.

Then the pressures of inflation and the prospect of future college bills caused Linda to decide it was time she found a job. There were few opportunities in her small suburban town, many in the city twenty miles away.

The Grahams sat down together and came to a decision. They are leaving their old life for the city, where child-care facilities are more plentiful, the children will be able to get around on their own on public transportation, Linda will find food stores and other shops in an easy walking radius of home and both parents will spend an extra hour morning and night with their families instead of on a commuter train.

"This kind of life-style no longer works for us," says Linda. "It doesn't fit the kind of life we want to lead today."

The Delsons next door, another family that used to fit the stereotypes, are remaining in their home, but inside the walls some major changes have taken place. Since she went to work, Marjorie Delson has little time for the home-baked cookies she used to make—so she has taught her children to bake for themselves.

"In this house now all four people clean and cook and wash dishes," she reports. "Two of us shop while the other two wash and iron. The kids cook every weekday evening. They have learned how to be independent. At twelve and fifteen, they take the commuter train to their dentist and and doctor appointments. They ride their bikes to swimming lessons and take responsibility for many of their own decisions. My husband has supported this change both physically and emotionally. There's no longer any reason why I must stay at home. The kids certainly don't."

"Suburban Lane," of course, is a fiction, but the Graham and Delson families are not. They represent thousands of families who have made practical changes to make their life-styles better fit their present needs. Each family's compromises are different, because they fit a different set of priorities and values.

Cindy and Lee Miller are young parents who have made another kind of choice. "We have decided that we will remain in an apartment rather than stretch to buy the house we used to dream about," Cindy states. "It is the only way we can afford for me to remain at home with the children until all three are in school. We talked a lot about it. It was not an easy choice, but we felt it was best for the children and my own peace of mind as well as Lee's. We can't help the cost of things today, but we can scale down our wants, get along with less to allow for values we feel are more important than trying to keep up with our friends."

Yes, the "typical American family" is changing—and perhaps it is a good thing. It is easy to look back with nostalgia on a family life that seems from our perspective to have been uncomplicated and serene, where husband and wife knew their places, marriages were stable and one kind of lifestyle seemed a proper goal for all.

But reality is seldom so simple. Few of us would choose to return to a time when women were restricted to their homes or when couples were forced by convention to stay bound for life in miserable marriages.

Living with other people has always required compromise. Parents have always had problems getting on with each other and guiding their children. The older generation has often thrown up its hands at the thought of the new world their children must face.

Our own lives have been complicated because the pace of outward change has speeded up, jostling many of our cherished definitions about family life. We have had to re-examine our roles and values in the light of new realities. Many marriages have foundered and many families have felt adrift in these confusing currents of change.

But the picture for the future is hopeful. In spite of the unrest of the past decade, 95 percent of us still choose to marry, and 80 percent of those who divorce marry again. And while they see a healthy new freedom in choosing a life path, most women still want children and most parents are still concerned most of all with raising those children to grow up healthy and happy and equipped to move out into the world on their own.

To accomplish this today may mean refusing to accept what have been established patterns. No one path works for every family any longer, and each of us must examine our own lives to determine the practical priorities that will best benefit those we live with and love. Even small changes can make a large difference.

For a while now we've lived in a world whose motto might have been, "Me First." Self-fulfillment and ways to assert ourselves have been common goals. Our family lives have sometimes been given second place to personal aspirations.

Not much as been written about it, but if you talk with people, there is a definite sense that commitment to family is coming back into fashion. A popular magazine runs an article called "Why Liberated Women Are Getting Married." A marriage counselor notes that the emphasis seems to be shifting toward saving rather than ending marriages. Divorce rates have slowed down a bit for the first time in many years. And corporations are reporting a reluctance among their executives to uproot their families for a job promotion. It used to be considered foolish to turn down a promotion, but enough people have begun doing so today to form what one psychologist calls "a critical mass that makes it OK to say maybe the family instead of the job comes first."

There is a growing reaffirmation of the importance of the family, a growing acknowledgment of author Michael Novak's observation, "If the quality of family life deteriorates, there is no quality of life."[22]

It remains for each of us to bring this affirmation into our own homes, to re-examine our lives and relationships and seek better ways to strengthen and preserve our most vital ties.

And we need to do something else, as well. We must remember that we are part of a larger family, too. It is natural that each of us is primarily concerned with our own problems, but we must not lose sight of how many of these problems we share with others.

Historian John Demos, a member of the Carnegie Council on Children and someone who has done much research into family life in the past, observes that the "crisis" of the family has been discussed in America for 150 years. But today's families do have a special problem, he feels, because we have lost so many of our reassuring ties. "The family has become our only setting for 'caring relationships,'" he says. "It is too much of a load for a family to carry. We need to defuse our caring lives, to spread our affection and concern to others. We can't become so closed off within our own four walls that we block off new opportunities for growth."

We've seen that many who are struggling with individual problems have found support and help from one another. If we will care more about other families, we may be able to work together to solve some of the larger problems that affect us all.

The quality of community life directly touches every household. While we may lack some of the long-term neighborhood ties enjoyed by past generations, we can resurrect some of that old community feeling by getting involved wherever we live today. We cannot evade responsibility if we care about our children—and their children. Everyone must be concerned about progressive child-care facilities for working mothers, centers where the elderly can be cared for without shutting them away from the rest of the world, housing where three generations may be able to know and help one another, better health care and better schools for all. We can't afford to leave these things to others; each one of us has to care.

None of these are easy problems, but it is important to remember that we have never been without problems. The biggest one facing most families right now is the runaway inflation that so often leaves mothers with no choice but to work to help support their families. As a society, we cannot afford to lose the benefits of the kind of warmth and consistency that used to be provided naturally by mothers at home. "The question is not whether women should be forced back into their homes or should have an equal say with men in world affairs," wrote Margaret Mead. "We urgently need to draw on the talents women have to offer. What we need to be sure of is that areas of caretaking associated in the past with families do not simply drop out of our awareness so that basic human needs go unmet."[23]

Time and energy have human limits. When a mother works, some of what she would like to give to her family must be curtailed. While there is a healthy trend toward fathers taking a larger role at home, realistically they cannot entirely fill the gap as our present working world operates.

Men have long given their prime energies to work and had little left over for their families. We are in danger of putting women into the same dilemma. After conforming for so long to the demands of the "real world" of work, both men and women concerned with family life must seek a better way.

Flexible hours, part-time jobs and new employment patterns that will allow time for family life are a beginning. They are a change from the work traditions of the past, but a change that seems a necessity for the well-being of the family of the future.

It won't be an easy task to accomplish, but we've seen that there is strength in numbers. So if a big enough family of parents makes itself heard, perhaps the business world will have to listen.

And perhaps we will discover anew what we once knew long ago: It is the family that is the real world, after all.

Chapter Notes

1. *Current Opinion*, Vol. II, Issue 6, June 1974, p. 64.
2. Demos, John, "The American Family in Past Time," *The American Scholar*, Summer 1974, p. 64.
3. U.S. Bureau of Labor Statistics.
4. Institute of Life Insurance, Washington, D.C.
5. *The New York Times*, July 30, 1979, ©1979 by The New York Times Company. Reprinted by permission.
6. Curtis, Jean, *Working Mothers*, p. 76.
7. *The New York Times*, January 28, 1978, ©1978 by The New York Times Company. Reprinted by permission.
8. *Marketing News*, January 28, 1977, p. 3.
9. *The New York Times*, October 28, 1977, ©1977 by The New York Times Company. Reprinted by permission.
10. *The New York Times*, November 27, 1977, ©1977 by The New York Times Company. Reprinted by permission.
11. Mace, David and Vera, *We Can Have Better Marriages If We Really Want Them*, Abingdon Press, 1974.
12. *The Joys and Sorrows of Parenthood*, Charles Scribner's Sons, pp. 63-64, ©1973 Group for the Advancement of Psychiatry.
13. *Ibid*, p. 61.
14. *Advocate of Stamford*, March 2, 1978.
15. *The New Extended Family*, p. 36, ©1977 by Ellen Galinsky and William H. Hooks. Used by permission of Houghton Mifflin Company.
16. *Christian Science Monitor*, Oct. 31, 1977.
17. *Advocate of Stamford*, March 2, 1978.
18. *Ibid*.
19. *The New York Times*, November 3, 1977, ©1977 by The New York Times Company. Reprinted by permission.
20. Despert, J. Louise, M.D., *Children of Divorce*, p. 14. copyright ©1963 by J. Louise Despert. Reprinted by permission of Doubleday & Company, Inc.
21. Aldridge, Leslie, *The Second Time Around*, p. 56, ©1977 by Leslie Aldridge Westoff. Reprinted by permission of Viking Penguin Inc.
22. Novak, Michael, "The Family Out of Favor," *Harper's Magazine*, April 1976, p. 44.
23. Mead, Margaret, *Aspects of the Present* by Margaret Mead and Rhoda Metraux, William Morrow, 1980.

Bibliography

Aldridge, Leslie, *The Second Time Around: Remarriage in America*, New York: Viking Press, 1977.

Bane, Mary Jo, *Here to Stay: American Families in the 20th Century*, New York: Basic Books, 1977.

Beck, Dorothy Fahs, *Marriage and the Family Under Challenge*, New York: Family Service Association of America, 1976.

Child Study Association of America, *Where We Are: A Hard Look at Family and Society*, New York: 1970.

Curtis, Jean, *Working Mothers*, New York: Doubleday, 1976.

Demos, John, "The American Family in Past Time," *The American Scholar*, Volume 43, Number 3, Summer 1974.

Despert, J. Louise, M.D., *Children of Divorce*, Dolphin Books, Doubleday & Company, Inc., Garden City, New York, 1962.

Dyer, William G., *Creating Closer Families*, Provo, Utah: Brigham Young University Press, 1975.

Galinsky, Ellen and Hooks, William H., *The New Extended Family: Day Care That Works*, Boston: Houghton Mifflin, 1977.

Gardner, Richard A., *The Parents' Book About Divorce*, New York: Doubleday, 1977.

Goodman, Elaine and Walter, *The Family: Yesterday, Today, Tomorrow*, New York: Farrar, Straus & Giroux, 1975.

Group for the Advancement of Psychiatry, Committee of Public Education, *The Joys and Sorrows of Parenthood*, New York: Charles Scribner's Sons, 1973.

Hope, Carol and Young, Nancy, *Momma, The Source Book for Single Mothers*, New York: New American Library, 1976.

Keniston, Kenneth and the Carnegie Council on Children, *All Our Children*, New York: Harcourt Brace Jovanovich, 1977.

Levine, James A., *Who Will Raise the Children?*, Philadelphia: J.B. Lippincott, 1976.

Mace, David and Vera, *We Can Have Better Marriages If We Really Want Them*, Nashville, Tennessee: Abingdon Press, 1974.

Rice, Robert M., *American Family Policy, Content and Context*, New York: Family Service Association of America, 1977.

Shorter, Edward, *The Making of the Modern Family*, New York: Basic Books, 1975.

Skolnick, Arlene S. and Jerome H., *The Fractured Family*, Boston: Little, Brown and Company, 1971.

Spock, Benjamin, *Raising Children in a Difficult Time*, New York: Pocket Books, 1976.

136

Index